Living Stones Pilgrimage

Living Stones Pilgrimage

With the Christians of the Holy Land

ALISON HILLIARD AND BETTY JANE BAILEY

CASSELL

Cassell
Wellington House, 125 Strand, London WC2R 0BB
www.cassell.co.uk

First published 1999

British Library Cataloguing-in-Publication Data
A catalogue record for this book is available from the British Library.

ISBN 0-304-70466-0

Photographs by Garo Nalbandian

The transcripts of a BBC World Service broadcast on pages 56–68 are
used by permission of the BBC.
Map on pages 128–9: Christian Information Centre, Jerusalem
See pages 130–2 for the copyright of individual hymns

Typeset by BookEns Ltd, Royston, Herts.
Printed and bound in Great Britain by
Biddles Ltd, Guildford and King's Lynn

Contents

Foreword

Come to him, a living stone, though rejected by mortals yet chosen and precious in God's sight, and like living stones, let yourselves be built into a spiritual house, to be a holy priesthood, to offer spiritual sacrifices acceptable to God through Jesus Christ.

(1 Peter 2:4–5)

On an early spring morning almost 2,000 years ago, the Holy Spirit descended on a small group of people who were gathered in a room in Jerusalem. It was *in* this place that those first followers of Jesus became the earliest witnesses to the Gospel of Christ, giving rise to what would become the Church. It was *from* this place that those witnesses went into all the world to share the good news of God in Christ Jesus, planting the seeds of the Kingdom of God wherever they journeyed.

Today here in the Holy Land, descendants of those first Christian witnesses are still to be found. The Christians of the Holy Land, the 'living stones', continue to bear testimony to the power, truth and love of the Gospel, as they have done faithfully and continuously throughout the last two millennia in this place of Jesus' birth, ministry, passion and resurrection.

The local Christian community, your brothers and sisters, wish to invite you to their land, to share with you their narrative and their heritage, to help you discover the land in which our common faith is still rooted. This book is designed to help you to respond to that invitation as you seek to experience the living faith of Jesus Christ in this holy land.

We greet you in Christian fellowship and hospitality. *Ahlan wa Sahlan*: you are most welcome here!

*But you will receive power when the Holy Spirit has come upon you;
and you will be my witnesses in Jerusalem, in all Judaea and
Samaria, and to the ends of the earth.*

(Acts 1:8)

✖ Michel Sabbah
Latin Patriarch of Jerusalem
President, Middle East Council of Churches
September 1998

Appreciation

This is a guidebook with a difference. It is more concerned with people than places. It is an invitation, not merely an explanation. It is written with a passion that stirs the heart of the reader. Its purpose is to transform Christian visitors into pilgrims by luring them off the tourist track into the company of Palestinian fellow-believers who trace their roots to the disciples of Jesus.

The introduction to the different churches in Jerusalem is written with the lucidity and accuracy that betray deep learning, but is infused with a warm sympathy that makes one want to experience liturgies fragrant with incense and framed by icons that glow and seem to move in the flames of flickering oil lamps.

The treatment of the holy places is infused with an astringent spirituality which makes it difficult for readers to remain on the surface of sites associated with Jesus both in Galilee and in Jerusalem. They are gently but firmly helped to give these places meaning in terms of their own lives by profound, pointed questions, key words designed to focus reflection, and suggestions for prayer. It would be hard to imagine a more effective antidote to the mawkish sentimentality that claims to evoke, but only succeeds in masking, the reality of Jesus' struggle.

This creative and timely book empowers pilgrims to reclaim in fellowship with Palestinian Christians the land in which the Word became flesh. It enables them to make it their spiritual home.

Jerome Murphy-O'Connor OP
Ecole Biblique, Jerusalem

Welcome

Ever since I assumed the directorship of the Jerusalem Liaison Office in late 1996, I have wanted to publish, under the name of the Middle East Council of Churches, an alternative guidebook that will not only complement our own ministry of ecumenical travel services, but also focus on the local Christians of the Holy Land. As a result, Alison and Betty co-authored this guidebook as an alternative resource for Christian pilgrims to the Holy Land. Ideally, it will be used alongside the numerous commercial guidebooks available on the market which contain an A to Z of holy sites, as well as basic information on travel and accommodation.

Christian pilgrimage is not new to the Holy Land! It has been going on since well before AD 333, the date of the first diary kept by a Christian pilgrim from Bordeaux. For centuries, pilgrims stayed in monasteries, convents or the homes of fellow-believers, sharing prayer and news, theological ideas and liturgical practices. Twentieth-century mass tourism, however, with its comfortable hotels, air-conditioned coaches and tightly packed schedules, transformed pilgrims into tourists, pilgrimages into holidays, and effectively hid the local Christian community from the visitor. Very few tour guides in Israel today are Palestinian – either Christian or Muslim. It is all too common to hear Christian Palestinians expressing both frustration and disappointment that Christians coming from abroad are either ignorant about the existence of indigenous Christians in the land where Christianity was born, or too busy visiting biblical sites to spend a few hours with those 'living stones' who trace their roots to Jesus' disciples and to the Church of the First Pentecost. After all, they say, Christianity is not frozen in a biblical time warp!

This book, then, is a guide to living Christianity in the Holy

Land, aiming to facilitate your contact with local Christians and to introduce you to some church traditions and practices you may not be familiar with. Unfamiliarity can lead to alienation, and I suggest that you read this guidebook to make yourself feel more at home with those who share your own faith within a different cultural setting.

Use it to meet local Christians and hear their stories of life in a troubled land. Although their numbers have dwindled in percentage terms over the last 50 years, there are today around 114,000 Christians in Israel proper and another 51,000 in the Occupied Palestinian territories. Altogether, Christians constitute just over 2.4 per cent of the overall population in the Holy Land. Listen to them talking about some of the hardships of daily life here and join with them as they worship together. They need your prayers and support, but they also need the reassurance that they have not become the forgotten faithful. Let them open their homes and churches to you and share with you some of the richness of their historical and contemporary witness to the Christian faith.

Included in this guidebook is a section on the major church denominations in Jerusalem, and then some alternative ways to go beyond the typical – commercial – purview of tourism. There are three walks within Jerusalem designed to make the old, traditional Christian pilgrimage routes more contemporary. Bethlehem is presented both as a biblical city and as a modern-day town preparing for the 2,000th anniversary of the birth of Jesus Christ. Sites around the Sea of Galilee are the inspiration for meditating on life today. Gaza is presented as an opportunity to discover how the churches and human rights organizations have responded to the contemporary Israeli–Palestinian conflict.

The section on towns and villages highlights areas rarely on a travel itinerary but with a significant Christian presence or important Christian institutions. Christian celebrations reflect a panoply of traditions known to those who live in the Holy Land but not always discovered by first-time travellers. Responsible shopping and bookstore listings allow you to return home with meaningful souvenirs.

In short, consider this guidebook as an invitation to an alternative encounter with the Holy Land and as an opportunity to enrich your own faith by sharing in the presence, life and witness of local Christians.

And as I invite you to the Holy Land, I would like to express my gratitude to all those who helped Alison and Betty with this guidebook – from the Church leadership to the Palestinian grassroots. A special word of thanks goes out to Christian Aid in London, one of our staunchest ecumenical partners, for helping us fund this guidebook and marketing it in the United Kingdom.

Salaam in *Shalom*.

Dr Harry Hagopian
Executive Director
Jerusalem Liaison Office

Introduction to the Jerusalem churches

Jerusalem is home to thirteen different churches or denominations that are considered traditional, ranging from the ancient churches of the East to the Protestants of the Reformation.

Many of its churches' traditions are unfamiliar to Western visitors who come to see the holy sites and end up running where Jesus walked, leaving no time to be spiritually enriched or challenged by the 'living stones' who live and worship in Jerusalem today. Often too, many pilgrims participate only in the acts of worship organized for their own tour group by a leader 'from home', and thus leave the city unaware of the diversity and richness of local Christian worship going on daily in churches throughout the Holy Land.

This guide to Jerusalem's churches is an introduction to the main church denominations in the city, sharing a little of their history, their traditions and the buildings in which they worship. It is also designed to be an alternative and a more authentic way of exploring Jerusalem and its holy sites.

The larger number of Palestinian Christians are Orthodox, dividing into either Oriental Orthodox or Eastern Orthodox. The separation of the two Orthodox families arose out of a disagreement in the fifth century over how to define the human and divine natures of Christ. The Eastern Orthodox accepted the definition proposed at the Fourth Ecumenical Council of Chalcedon in 451 that Christ was two eternally inseparable natures, both human and divine. The Oriental Orthodox rejected the council's definition in favour of other definitions of the nature of Christ and became known as non-Chalcedonian Orthodox, or

Monophysites (one nature-ites). The Oriental Orthodox are not in communion with either Constantinople (Greek Orthodoxy) or Rome. Today, however, the theological differences between the Oriental and Eastern Orthodox have largely been overcome and the two families are divided more for historic than doctrinal reasons.

The Orthodox tradition may be unfamiliar to you. If it is, introduce yourself to a new way of worshipping, using icons, incense, ceremonial and meditative prayer. Feast your senses on the bright colours and rich decoration of the places of prayer which for centuries have been hallowed by worship into sacred spaces where heaven and earth meet.

Begin with the Greek Catholic (Melkite) Church just inside Jaffa Gate (page 35). Although it is Catholic, in communion with Rome, it is a good entry point into the Orthodox tradition, faithfully following most of the Eastern Orthodox practices. It is, for example, one of the best places to learn how to read the iconography so loved by Orthodox Christians.

Icons are meant to be like open books that remind us of God and that give visual form to doctrines of the church. They are not worshipped but they point to God and help make God's acts known to the world. They are also considered 'thin places', where the persons and events pictured are present to the believer in the here and now. The icon therefore becomes a two-way window into the world of the Spirit – into the Kingdom of God, reminding the worshipper of the great company of Christians in all times and places who are still present as they worship God.

Go along to a local service – there is usually at least one every day in every church. (Information on times is available from the Christian Information Centre near Jaffa Gate: see page 125. Note that the times can change for summer and winter. The CIC has an accurate list of service times.) Stop and talk to those who are the descendants of the Church of the First Pentecost and whose ancestors have lived and worshipped here for centuries.

If you go to worship remember to dress modestly, covering your arms and wearing loose trousers or a modest skirt. Expect to stand. The absence of pews or seats in a large number of

Orthodox churches demonstrates a flexible worship, an informality whereby people can come and go freely, accommodating personal piety as well as community worship. People here are at home in their church.

The liturgy itself is seen as the meeting place between doctrine and worship. It is the vehicle which forms the bridge between heaven and earth, bringing the transcendent God and humanity into contact with each other. It is an unhurried and timeless experience of heaven and earth in the company of God, all the angels and all the saints.

Services can last for up to four hours – this is time outside earthly constraints! It is not rude, however, to leave. Light a candle and say a prayer before you go.

The liturgy is mostly drawn from the words of Scripture and is sung or chanted. Singing is the way Orthodox Christians pray in church. It is the way the church worships. The language and the melodies may be strange to you. Lose the quest to know and understand everything. Instead, allow the music to be your passport into this ageless experience, stilling you to reflection and meditation.

If you would like to organize more formal meetings with local churches and their members, there are details on pages 126–7 of organizations which can help. Also included is a telephone and fax contact point for each church if you want more information on times of services, opening hours or to set up your own encounter.

The memories and insights you gain from these experiences are to be found in no guidebook. It is the faith of local Christians, after all, which breathes life into dead stones.

Armenian Orthodox Church

After Armenia became the first nation to adopt Christianity as a state religion in AD 301, Armenian Christian pilgrims began to travel to the Holy Land. Many settled in the south-east side of the ancient city, which is now the Armenian quarter, forming about one-sixth of the Old City. Armenians claim to have the longest uninterrupted presence in Jerusalem and the Armenian Church is one of the three guardians of the Holy Places, along with the Greek Orthodox and the Franciscan Holy Custody (Catholics).

The early Armenian pilgrims built the first Armenian church in Jerusalem in the fourth century, St James's Cathedral. Today's present cathedral is built on the site of the original church. It is erected over the place where the head of St James, the apostle of Jesus, is said to be buried. He was martyred in AD 44 and is today the patron saint of Armenians. The Cathedral is named after that St James, and also after St James, the brother of the Lord, who was appointed as the first Christian Bishop of Jerusalem after Christ's ascension to heaven. His relics are buried under the main altar of the church.

Today's cathedral, at the entrance to the Armenian convent area, is a marriage of Crusader and Armenian architecture – the dome, for example, is typical of a tenth-century church in Armenia. It faces east, as do all Armenian churches, and is built in such a way that the sun does not set in the church. Its small windows allow it to receive natural light from morning to late afternoon and spectacular shafts of sunlight regularly flood the church. All the prayers in the church are therefore in daylight with the sun seen to symbolize the light of life and the nature of God. Vespers are from 3 p.m. to 3.30 p.m., the only weekday time the

Cathedral is open to tourists or pilgrims. Talk with one of the priests after the liturgy.

Most Armenian churches have little adornment. St James's, however, is richly decorated with carpets, lamps and icons given by visiting pilgrims. Distinctive Armenian blue-green ceramic tiles cover most of the lower parts of the walls. These were crafted by a single Armenian family in Kutahya in Turkey. Ten thousand of them were then brought to Jerusalem over 200 years ago to decorate the Armenian holy places in the Holy Land. Some of the tiles are pictorial, depicting great biblical scenes from Adam and Eve to the Last Supper and the lives of the saints. All have a cross hidden somewhere in their design, reflecting the centrality of Christianity to the Armenian identity. The Armenian stone cross or *khatchkar* can be seen on the outside of the church and on the walls of the convent where thousands of them have been etched by visiting pilgrims wishing to be remembered. Some of the crosses date back to the ninth and tenth centuries.

Try and attend Vespers or Sunday Eucharist at 8.30 a.m. and listen to the fine choir of seminarians and its cantor. The seminarians come from Armenia and fill the church with music that often seems be caught up heavenward in the incense-laden shafts of sunlight. Singing is here a way of praying and giving glory to God. At its best this can be a mystical experience, a time for reflection, contemplation and closeness to God.

Notice the distinctive triangular black head-dresses or hoods worn by the priests, shaped like the typical dome of an Armenian church. The Armenian priest's dress and hood are designed to make him look like a walking Armenian church; symbolically, therefore, a walking church in this world.

The Cathedral of St James is the central feature of the compound of the Armenian monastery, which is like a city in miniature with its own school, library, seminary and residential quarters.

The parish church for local Armenians, the Church of the Archangels, is just past St James's Cathedral in an area known as the Convent of the Olive Tree. It is not open to the public. To the side of the church is an ancient olive tree. Tradition says it was the tree to which Jesus was tied and tortured, before he came before the High Priest Annas, whose house is said to have been on this site. The archangels, Gabriel and Michael, are said to have covered their faces with their wings to avoid seeing Christ being abused. Thus the church gets its name. The olive tree has come to be seen as a miracle-working tree. It is said, for example, that eating the fruit of the tree allows women who have difficulty getting pregnant to conceive.

Built into the north-east corner of the church is a stone, reputed to be one of the stones that would have cried out had the multitude of disciples not praised God on Palm Sunday (Luke 19:40).

Today there are about 2,000 Armenians in Jerusalem, around half of whom live in the Armenian quarter. After the Armenian genocide of 1915 in Ottoman Turkey, in which it is claimed more than one and a half million Armenians were killed, 20,000 Armenians fled to the Holy Land. Ten thousand of them sought refuge in the convent itself. Some of the survivors of the genocide still live there today. The memory of the genocide is kept alive every year by special services on 24 April and it is chronicled in the Convent's museum, which is open to the public.

Here is documentary photographic evidence of the genocide and of the history of the Armenian people and Armenia, now an independent republic of the former Soviet Union. There are also exhibits of the first printing press in Jerusalem, which Armenians brought to the city in the 1830s to produce liturgical books. Likewise an Armenian, who later became Patriarch of Jerusalem, introduced photography to the city. Many of his photographs are on display as well as archaeological finds made in the Armenian compound and brilliantly coloured illuminated manuscripts.

The entrance to the Mardigian Museum of Armenian History and Art is just past the Convent entrance on the left on Armenian Orthodox Patriarchate Road. It is open from 10 a.m. to 4 p.m. and closed on Sundays.

Contact point *Armenian Patriarchate: tel. 02-628 2331, fax 02-626 4861*

Note: when dialling from outside the country, replace the initial 0 with 00972; thus the numbers above become 00972-2-628 2331 and 00972-2-626 4861.

Syrian Orthodox Church

Jerusalem's small Syrian Orthodox Christian community is particularly proud of its heritage. The word 'Syrian' does not refer to the location of the church but rather to its use of the Syriac Aramaic language, a dialect of the language Jesus spoke in first-century Palestine. Syrian Christians see themselves as the first people to adopt Christianity as natives of the Holy Land: the historical Syria at the time of Christ included today's Syria, Lebanon, Jordan, Iraq, part of Turkey and most of what has been known as Palestine since AD 135. The Syrian Orthodox Church is possibly, therefore, the oldest Christian denomination of Semitic origin in the Middle East, and the Apostle Peter is considered to have been appointed its first Patriarch in AD 37.

The Syrian Orthodox church, St Mark's, and its convent are between the Armenian and Jewish Quarters on Ararat Road. The church is open from 9 a.m. to noon and from 3 p.m. to 5 p.m. and closed on Sundays. Vespers is daily at 4 p.m. in winter, 5 p.m. in summer.

St Mark's is said to be built on the site where Christians first gathered in Jerusalem, dating back to AD 73. Syrian Orthodox Christians claim it is also where Christ held the Last Supper, washed his disciples' feet and where the Pentecost took place with the Holy Spirit descending on the Apostles after Christ's ascension to heaven. Supporting that claim is a sixth-century inscription carved in Aramaic on the northern pillar inside the entrance of the church declaring this to be the home of St Mark and the home of Jesus' mother, Mary, after the death of Christ. A painting on leather of the Virgin and Child, said to be painted by St Luke the Evangelist, who was a painter and a physician, is now enshrined on the right hand side of the church as an icon. The portrait is placed just above the font which is, in turn, linked with a tradition which says that the Virgin Mary was baptized here by the Apostles.

Tradition also says this church is the place Peter went to when an angel released him from prison (Acts 12:12).

The icon of the Virgin Mary is much venerated today. Legend has it that the icon was stolen and returned to the church by itself. A similar protection is claimed for the holy liturgical manuscripts on display – some of them over 1,000 years old and still used in the daily worship in the church.

In addition to the services in St Mark's, Vespers are held in St Nicodemus Chapel in the Holy Sepulchre on Sundays at 8.30 a.m., and in the Tomb of the Virgin Mary on Wednesdays at 8 a.m.

There are only 500–700 Syrian Orthodox Christians in Jerusalem today. Before 1948 and the creation of the State of Israel, there were around 6,000 families. Like all other Christian traditions in the Holy Land, many have emigrated and much of the community's property was confiscated for Jewish expansion in 1967. There are currently around 6,000 Syrian Orthodox Christians in the Holy Land, most of them living in the Bethlehem area. Great pride is taken in the large Syrian Orthodox Scout group whose bagpipe playing can be heard at many Christian functions and processions.

Contact points
Syrian Orthodox Patriarchate: tel. 02-628 3304
Syrian Orthodox Patriarchal Vicar: tel. 02-628 8398, fax 02-627 7024

Ethiopian Orthodox Church

The Ethiopians trace their link with Jerusalem back 3,000 years to when the Ethiopian Queen of Sheba is said to have visited King Solomon in Jerusalem. This visit is twice referred to in the Bible (1 Kings 10:1–10, 1 Chronicles 9:1–9) but legend has embellished the story into the tradition that the Queen not only adopted King Solomon's faith during her six-month stay but returned to Ethiopia pregnant with his child. There she gave birth to a son, Menelik, meaning 'son of the King'.

When Menelik was 22 years old, his mother is said to have sent him to Jerusalem to meet his father. He stayed in Jerusalem for three years and, before his departure, Solomon crowned him King of Ethiopia and sent him home with numerous believing Jews, including priests from the Temple of Jerusalem.

Those Jews who accompanied him back to Ethiopia took not only their faith, but also their instruments of worship from the Temple in Jerusalem, such as the Temple rhythm instruments and drums. Similar drums are one of the most distinctive features of Ethiopian Christian worship today, used on special occasions and at times of great celebration.

According to tradition, some of the Ethiopians who travelled with the Queen of Sheba settled in the city. Many others came to Jerusalem after Christianity was introduced into Ethiopia, 34 years after the ascension of Christ, by the Ethiopian eunuch of Queen Candace of Ethiopia (Acts 8:26–40). He had come to Jerusalem to worship and, as finance minister, to supervise the royal possessions in Gaza. On his return from Jerusalem he was baptized by the Apostle Philip and, in turn, introduced baptism into Ethiopia.

The largest Ethiopian church in Jerusalem is the Dabra

Gannat Monastery on Ethiopia Street, just off Prophet's Street. Here the feasts and festivals of the Virgin Mary are celebrated. Go along and hear the girls' choir. Dressed in brilliant red, yellow, orange and green uniforms, they sing and process around the church beating their drums. Members of the congregation follow, draped in their traditional white robes, clapping, swaying and ululating in a blend of African, Hebrew and Christian traditions.

Ethiopian churches, like this one, are often round, with the sanctuary in the centre containing a *tabot* or sacred tablet of wood, symbolizing the Ark of the Covenant. Tradition says that the Ark was brought to Ethiopia by King Menelik. The tabot honours the Virgin Mary as the Ark of the New Covenant. Vespers are held daily in the church at 4 p.m.

The Ethiopians also have two chapels in the Holy Sepulchre itself, although their ownership is disputed by the Coptic Orthodox Church. Access to both is through a door to the right of the main entrance to the Holy Sepulchre. One is the Chapel of St Michael, the other is the Chapel of the Four Living Creatures which leads out onto the roof of the Holy Sepulchre. In this chapel, a large, brightly painted modern oil painting on the wall tells the story of King Solomon receiving the Queen of Sheba in Jerusalem. The King stands near his throne, a prominent Star of David on his chest. Behind him are Jewish sages, with the black garb and hair-curls of today's ultra-orthodox Jews.

Ethiopian Orthodox Christians are proud of their Jewish roots and links with Jerusalem. Jerusalem, they say, is like a stamp on their hearts as the cradle of their faith. Many Ethiopian women, for example, are baptized with the name Jerusalem.

Certain Ethiopian customs, such as circumcision, still follow Jewish practice today. Newborn boys, for example, are commonly circumcised on the eighth day after birth, as an initiation into the 'Covenant of Abraham'. (Following African tradition, newborn girls are also circumcised – on the fifth day.) In addition to their own dietary laws for their numerous days of fasting, Ethiopian Christians also observe a number of Old Testament dietary laws – it is forbidden, for example, to eat pork. In its beliefs and doctrine, however, the Ethiopian Church is entirely Christian Orthodox.

Moving from the chapel out onto the roof of the Holy Sepulchre takes you to the Ethiopian monastery where monks live in a honeycomb of small whitewashed cells or mud huts. The area is called the Convent of Deir-es-Sultan and there has been a convent here since at least 1530. In fact, this is said to be the place where Abraham prepared to sacrifice Isaac and instead found a ram in an olive tree. Today, about twenty monks live in this monastery.

Before the narrow entrance into the monastery is the dome or cupola in the middle of the courtyard. The cupola admits light to the crypt of St Helena's below and each year a large tent is erected here during the Holy Week of Easter to accommodate the many Easter pilgrims who arrive from Ethiopia.

Some of the great annual church feasts take place around this dome, like the Feast of the Holy Cross on 27 September. It is one of the most colourful and noisy celebrations in Jerusalem. On the eve, a fire is lit on the roof and the choir, singing and drumming, lead worshippers for several hours around the dome. Another colourful celebration takes place here on the evening of Holy Saturday called 'The Resurrection Procession' with the singing of Easter hymns by candlelight.

The worship is in Ge'ez – the liturgical language of Ethiopian Christians and a product of the Hebrew and Arabic languages. Five celebrants are required for the Eucharist, in which fresh warm bread is used.

All official liturgical prayers are ended by repeating two prayers: 'Lord Christ have mercy on us' and 'For the sake of Mary, Christ have mercy on us'. Each prayer is said twelve times. Ethiopian Christians count the twelve repetitions on the twelve joints of their four fingers. You can see them at speed going up and down the joints on their fingers from one hand to another at the end of every service.

There are around 2,000 Ethiopian Christians in the Holy Land. Around 70 monks and nuns live in monastic communities, but there are many immigrant workers or pilgrims who stay for some time.

Contact point *Ethiopian Orthodox Patriarchate: tel. 02-628 2848/628 6871, fax 02-626 4189/625 9652*

Coptic Orthodox Church

The Coptic Orthodox Church traces its founding back to St Mark and is the largest Christian church in the Middle East today. There are now around 2,000 Copts in the Holy Land. Many are originally from Egypt. The word Copt, in fact, derives from the Greek word *Aigyptos*, meaning Egyptian, and is used for all Egyptian Christians.

The Coptic Orthodox Church takes pride in its country's place in the Bible. Egypt is mentioned in the lives of Abraham, Joseph, Jacob, Moses and Jeremiah and there were residents of Egypt present in Jerusalem at the day of Pentecost. The Coptic Church is especially proud that Egyptian hospitality housed the Holy Family in its flight from Herod.

The story of that flight is told in the wall-size pictures depicting the life of Jesus in the community's main church, St Anthony's, close to the roof of the Holy Sepulchre.

The church is named after St Anthony the Great, the founder of monasticism in Egypt and one of the earliest Christian monks to live in the desert. Monks have been following in his footsteps and coming from Egypt to the Holy Land to establish monastic communities since the third and fourth centuries.

St Anthony has also given Coptic monks in Jerusalem their distinctive black cotton hoods or head-dresses. Tradition relates that an angel asked St Anthony to wear the headcovering, shaped like a baby's bonnet, to remind him to be simple and pure like a child. The devil, however, tried to pull the headcovering off. St Anthony caught it, ripping it down the middle. Today, the headcovering is stitched down the centre where the fabric has been torn in two, symbolizing the conflict between good and bad, the devil and God, that still continues in the world.

On the crown of the headcovering are twelve embroidered Coptic crosses – representing the twelve apostles and reminding monks to follow their teachings. Another cross is embroidered at the back – again symbolically placed to show that monks must leave everything earthly behind and only look to God as their goal.

The black cotton hoods are also worn by Syrian Orthodox monks. A hood is symbolic of monkhood in the Orthodox tradition.

The Coptic cross is also of distinctive design. It has three heads on each of its four arms, to represent the twelve apostles, with Christ at the centre.

A cross with a loop on top, called the ankh, is also common. It was used in Pharaonic art as a symbol of eternal life and has been adapted to Christian symbolism.

The liturgy is in the Coptic language and also in Arabic. As in all Orthodox Churches, there are many fast days – a legacy of its monastic tradition. Some degree of fasting is observed for 210 days a year, usually eliminating meat, fish and/or all dairy products plus wine and oil, and including total fasting for part of the day. There are fasts for 43 days before Christmas and eight weeks before Easter.

The Coptic Communion bread is called *corba*. It is leavened bread and it is baked in an oven by the church while psalms are sung. The thirteen crosses imprinted on the bread again symbolize Jesus and his disciples.

Today the Copts also look after St Helena's Chapel on the roof of the Holy Sepulchre. The chapel leads down some steep steps to St Helena's cistern, a cave-like space from which rain water was taken to help build the Holy Sepulchre. In winter it is full to overflowing and the steps are slippery – take care!

Outside the chapel is the Ninth Station of the Cross on the Via Dolorosa, where Christ fell for the third time under the cross.

The Coptic Pope in Egypt has ruled that no Egyptian pilgrims should take Communion in Jerusalem until the resolution of the church's property dispute with the Israeli government over ownership of the two chapels in the Holy Sepulchre.

Contact point *Coptic Orthodox Patriarchate: tel. 02-627 2645, fax 02-627 2773*

Greek Orthodox Church

The Greek Orthodox Church is the largest faith community in the Holy Land with about 60,000 members.

The Church dates itself back to the Apostle James who was the first Bishop of Jerusalem. In New Testament times, Greek culture was predominant in the eastern regions of the Roman Empire and many of the gentiles whom Paul converted were of that Greek culture. Ever since AD 451, except during the Crusades, Jerusalem has been a Patriarchate of the Greek Orthodox Church and the Greek Patriarch has the status of 'first' when the church leaders in Jerusalem meet.

The Jerusalem Patriarchate is one of the three guardians of the Holy Places, through its Brotherhood of the Holy Sepulchre. The Patriarch, the upper hierarchy, and the Brotherhood are almost all Greeks, while the parish priests and lay people are Arabs. The Byzantine liturgy is celebrated in Greek in the monasteries and Arabic in the parish churches.

Visits to many Greek Orthodox churches, apart from the public Holy Places, need to be arranged by special appointment.

A short cut to gain some insight into the traditions of the Church is a brief visit to the museum of the Greek Orthodox Patriarchate. It is open to the public daily from 9.30 a.m. to 1 p.m. and is on Greek Orthodox Patriarchate Road.

The museum is in the grounds of the Patriarchate itself and, with its olive, orange and lemon trees and rose gardens, it is an oasis of calm in a busy city.

There has been a museum here since 1858. This new collection, however, houses manuscripts, historical documents and samples of the Patriarchate's religious and artistic treasures. There are, for example, parts of the tomb of King Baldwin V from the Church of the Holy Sepulchre in 1186, sarcophagi from the family tomb of Herod the Great in the first century BC and illustrated manuscripts of the Gospel from the twelfth century.

St John the Baptist Church

This is said to be one of the oldest churches in Jerusalem, originally built in the mid-fifth century, and is today below street level. Tradition claims this was the House of Zebedee, father of James and John.

The church, on Christian Quarter Road, is almost entirely covered in frescoes, painted by two nuns, also blood sisters, from Athens who came to Jerusalem in the early 1990s. The two sisters travel from one Greek Orthodox church to another helping to restore icons and frescoes.

Many of the frescoes depict scenes in the life of John the Baptist. On the right hand side inside the main door, for example, is an icon depicting the severed head of St John. There is also a relic of his bones, decorated with silver and precious stones. Many people come here to venerate the saint's holy bones – for example, placing injured parts of their own body on the relic while praying for restoration to health.

Also worth noting is the rotunda of the church, similar to the splendid new dome of the Church of the Holy Sepulchre, with its stars and rays symbolizing the light of Christ.

There are services in this church every Wednesday morning in winter time and on all the feast days of St John the Baptist.

The church is the focus of the Order of St John's Hospitallers, familiar to British visitors in its modern manifestation as the St John's Ambulance Brigade.

St James's Church

On the left side of the parvis (courtyard) of the Holy Sepulchre, several chapels belong to the Greek Orthodox. Mar Yacoub, or St James, is today the parish church for the Arabic-speaking Greek Orthodox of the Old City.

St Onuphrius Monastery

This monastery, close to Silwan village in the valley of Gehenna, is currently being renovated by a small group of Greek Orthodox sisters after years of disuse. To get there, go past the Abu-Tor Observatory on the Hebron Road and turn right down Ha-Mefakked Street. The entrance is on a narrow road on the right near the bottom of the valley. It is easily missed!

A monastery was first established here in the nineteenth century. It was named after St Onuphrius, a fourth-century saint and the son of a Persian king, who came to Jerusalem as a pilgrim. As a young man, influenced by John the Baptist, he went to live in the desert in Egypt. From there he travelled to Jerusalem and lived for several years in a cave which is now the church of the monastery.

Desert dwellers like St Onuphrius would look for places to live which were cursed in the hope that their presence and prayers would bring God into that place and force any evil spirits to leave.

The area on which the monastery is built had such a reputation. It is known as the Potter's Field or the Field of Blood – so called either because the Chief Priests bought it with the 30 pieces of blood money as a burial place for strangers (Matthew 27:7–10) or because Judas, who had bought the field, committed suicide there after betraying Jesus (Acts 1:18–19).

The cave where Onuphrius lived is also said to be the cave in which the Apostles hid in fear when Christ was crucified. It was originally a grave tomb as the area was a cemetery. In fact, the whole hillside is honeycombed with tombs, many examples of which are visible inside the monastery today. Some are empty. Others are stacked high with the dry bones of thousands of pilgrims who came to Jerusalem at the beginning of the century and who never made the return journey home – a visible commentary on the perils of pilgrimage a century ago.

Inside the monastery's church is an icon of St Onuphrius – a strange-looking figure covered almost entirely in hair. Tradition relates that when he was in the desert he prayed that God would clothe him. His prayers were answered when hair – like fur – grew on his body and his beard reached down to his ankles.

The nuns pray in this cave three times a day, beginning at 3.30 a.m. Much of the rest of their time is spent tending the monastery's garden which has recently been planted with vegetables, flowers and vines. They see their work as transforming this place into a taste of paradise, reminding people of what heaven will be like.

They can provide accommodation and wonderful hospitality for a small number of pilgrims and have special services on 12 June – the feast day of St Onuphrius, who is today reputed to come to the help of those travelling by sea and those who are having difficulty in court cases.

Contact point *Greek Orthodox Patriarchate: tel./fax 02-628 2048*

Russian Orthodox Church

B yzantine Orthodox Christianity became the state religion in Russia in AD 988. During the eleventh century, Russian pilgrims began to make their way to the Holy Land, but they did not establish their own institutions in Palestine until the nineteenth century, when pilgrims started to come in their thousands to Jerusalem.

Russian pilgrimage, unlike that of some countries, was a phenomenon of the poor peasants. The pilgrims spent months collecting money for the trip and then travelled by foot and boat to reach Jaffa, where they continued their trek to Jerusalem by the cheapest transportation available – donkey. They often stayed from Advent to Easter, bringing gifts from their home town and collecting souvenirs and relics to take back. The pilgrimage itself was looked on as preparation for death in the hope of resurrection, so sometimes one old man or woman would go representing the entire village. Pilgrims brought back earth to be sprinkled on their coffin, blessed crosses to wear around the neck and a shroud that had been placed on the stone of unction in the Holy Sepulchre.

After the Crimean War, when the number of pilgrims made a dramatic increase and the Tsar was eager to increase his influence in the region, 32 acres of choice real estate were acquired by the Russians. Construction began on the northern plateau outside the Old City Walls in 1860. The area, known today as the Russian Compound, contained several large hospices, a hospital, a consulate and a cathedral.

The Russian Revolution of 1917 and its disdain of the Church put an end to pilgrimage and also gave rise to a 'Church in Exile' – also called 'The Church Abroad' – with its headquarters in New

York. The continuing Patriarchate in Moscow is called 'The Moscow Patriarchate'.

Both groups hold property and churches in Jerusalem and, since the collapse of Communism and the greater openness to the Christian faith in Russia, there has been increased dispute over ownership and who is the authentic voice of Russian Orthodoxy in the Holy Land. The two main churches of the Church Abroad are in Gethsemane and on the Mount of Olives and there is another in the Christian Quarter near the Holy Sepulchre. The main church of the Moscow Patriarchate is the Holy Trinity Cathedral, in the Russian Compound, an area today commonly associated with the headquarters of Jerusalem's district police and its prison.

THE CHURCH ABROAD

The Convent of the Ascension

This convent is close to the Mount of Olives Hotel, next to the Mount of Olives Bus Company. It is only open to the public on Tuesdays and Thursdays from 9 a.m. to 12 noon. Vespers are daily at 4 p.m. (Don't confuse it with the Church of the Ascension on the grounds of Augusta Victoria Hospital.)

The convent is set in grounds which house the Church of the Ascension, a bell tower, the chapel where St John the Baptist's head was found, a library, a refectory, nuns' cells and a pilgrimage hostel.

The pilgrimage hostel started in the last century to cater for the tens of thousands of Russian pilgrims who came to Jerusalem. Some women pilgrims decided to remain and live monastically as a community, and the consecration of the convent was performed in 1906. In 1917, around 300 nuns lived here. Today there are only about 60, of ten different nationalities. They all share the task of looking after the convent. Some paint icons, make pressed flower cards, prayer ropes or painted eggs which are for sale at the entrance. Others look after the convent's many olive trees; the olives are salted to eat or pressed for oil and used to light the many oil lamps in the churches.

The Church of the Ascension

This is a typical Byzantine church, cruciform in shape and with one large cupola. It was built by the Russian Imperial House and consecrated in 1886. The first church on this site was built in the fourth century, under the instructions of the Empress Helena from Constantinople who came to Jerusalem, found the cross on which Christ was crucified and had churches built all over Palestine. Some evidence of the original church can be seen, such as the original broken marble floor in the middle of the church.

The church was built to commemorate the ascension of Christ from the Mount of Olives. (The traditional site of the ascension is about 200 metres outside the convent and is today under Muslim control.)

One icon in the church is especially loved – the icon of the Mother of God called 'Quick to Hear'. This is on your right as you enter the church, and many of the nuns say they receive help from this icon today, turning to it in times of distress. It has been venerated in this way since 1914, when the young novices who were left in the convent at the outbreak of the First World War gathered around it every evening, praying for protection and help.

There are services in the church twice a day – 5.30 a.m. in summertime, 6 a.m. in wintertime and 4 p.m. every afternoon. The services are conducted in old Church Slavonic.

Just behind the church is a chapel, built on the site where the head of St John the Baptist is said to have been discovered. Tradition says that Joanna, one of the women who brought spices to the tomb and a follower of Christ, recovered St John's head from a rubbish heap where it had been thrown and buried it in a clay pot on the Mount of Olives. St John is then said to have appeared in the fourth century in a dream to two Syrian monks who had come to Jerusalem as pilgrims. He came to them three times showing them where the head was buried and insisted they go and find it. They did. St Helena heard of their discovery and ordered that a chapel be built to cover the holy site. A hole covered with a grill today marks the site.

The current chapel was built in 1922, although some of the remains of the first chapel can still be seen, including a well-preserved mosaic with birds, fruits and St Peter's fish. Services are held here on the feast days of St John. The Psalter is also read continuously in this chapel in memory of the departed, and prayers are said for their souls as they move from one world to the next.

Outside the chapel, to the left, are carob trees, also known as locust trees, with their ugly brown–black edible pods called St John's bread or locust fruit. Many believe this is what St John actually ate along with wild honey in the desert – not the locust/grasshoppers Western Christians imagine. The confusion, it seems, stems from a translation error, since in Aramaic, the language of first-century Palestine, the word 'locust' referred either to the fruit of the locust tree or to a grasshopper.

To your left is the Church of the Ascension's Bell Tower. The cross on this tower marks the highest point in Jerusalem and you can hear the sisters ring the bell from here every morning and afternoon and before each service.

The four-ton bell was a gift from Russia: it arrived by sea to the port of Jaffa in the 1870s. Tradition reports that it was transported to the Mount of Olives by 150 women forming teams to pull it on a platform all the way to Jerusalem! The journey, not surprisingly, took weeks.

Contact point *Tel. 02-628 4373, fax 02-628 2367*

The Russian Orthodox Convent of Saint Mary Magdalene

This convent is further down the Mount of Olives in the Garden of Gethsemane. With its seven golden onion-shaped domes, the main church is one of the most distinctive landmarks of Jerusalem.

The church was built by Tsar Alexander III in 1888 and is

dedicated to Mary Magdalene. There are scenes from her life painted on murals all around the church. The large canvas above the iconostasis shows Mary Magdalene before the Roman Emperor Tiberius. In her hand she holds a red egg which she presents to the Emperor. The red symbolizes the spilling of Christ's blood and his death on the cross; the egg symbolizes the Resurrection and new life. This is the Christian origin of the Orthodox tradition of having painted eggs for Easter.

The other focal point of the church is the main icon to the front of the church, on the right side of the iconostasis, or icon screen. It is an icon of the Mother of God of Smolensk – Hodigitria – and is credited with working miracles ever since it was brought to the church in 1939 from Lebanon. It had survived a fire in a village church there in the sixteenth century and in this century it had been given to the local Metropolitan. He was told in a dream to give the icon to the first abbess of St Mary Magdalene Monastery in Jerusalem which had just been founded.

The church also houses the relics of Saint Elizabeth who, as Grand Duchess Serge of Russia, presided at the church's consecration in 1888. After her husband was assassinated in 1905 she became a nun and founded a convent dedicated to works of charity in Moscow. After the revolution in 1917, she and another nun, Barbara, were thrown down a mine shaft by the Bolsheviks and left to die. Her remains and those of Sister Barbara were eventually rescued and transported to Jerusalem in 1920. Both women were canonized in 1981. Saint Elizabeth is a popular saint in Russia and her relics are greatly venerated by the many Russian pilgrims who come to Jerusalem.

Princess Andrew of Greece, mother of the Duke of Edinburgh, Prince Philip, visited the church and stayed in the monastery in the 1930s. She later became a nun and wished to be buried near her aunt, the Grand Duchess Elizabeth. In 1988, her remains were transferred to a crypt below the church.

The church is a place of daily worship for the women's convent of St Mary Magdalene. Vespers are daily at 4.30 p.m.; liturgy is at 5 a.m. on weekdays and at 7 a.m. on Sundays. Services are open to pilgrims for worship, but not to tourists. You can visit the church on Tuesdays and Thursdays from 10 a.m. to 12 noon.

During the year there are other special services open to the public, such as the Feast of St Mary Magdalene on 4 August or on the feast day of the icon of the Mother of God of Smolensk on 10 August.

Today, the convent is home to 28 nuns from all over the world. Their work of hand-painted Russian eggs and icons, prayer ropes, embroidery and handmade incense is for sale at the monastery kiosk below the church.

Contact point *Tel. 02-628 4371, fax 02-628 6381*

St Alexander's Chapel

In 1859, the Russian consul acquired a valuable piece of property near the Church of the Holy Sepulchre and across the Suq from the Redeemer Lutheran Church. While digging for the foundations, some interesting ruins were uncovered. Named after St Alexander Nevsky, the church was built over and incorporated these ruins which are believed to be parts of the Second Old City Wall and the original church of the Holy Sepulchre.

Inside the Russian building there is a threshold which some believe to be part of the Judgement Gate which Jesus passed through on his way to Golgotha. If this is indeed the Gate and the Second Wall (which was built before the time of Jesus), it would be additional proof that the Holy Sepulchre is built over a spot which was outside the walls at the time of the crucifixion. The chapel itself is decorated with icons and large paintings but it is not always open to the public.

Contact point *Russian Ecclesiastical Mission of the Russian Church Abroad: tel. 02-628 3088, fax 02-628 6382*

THE MOSCOW PATRIARCHATE

Holy Trinity Cathedral

The main Russian Orthodox Patriarchate building is the Cathedral of the Holy Trinity. Its style is seventeeth-century Russian baroque with typical onion-shaped domes crowned with gold crosses.

Although meant to be open to the public every day from 9 a.m. to 1 p.m., it is often locked. In summertime, services are held on Saturdays at 5 p.m. and on Sundays at 8 a.m. A growing number of Russian immigrants attend.

Wintertime services are held in the first Russian Orthodox church to be built in Jerusalem, the Church of the Patriarchate, St Alexandra's Church. It is just to the side of the Cathedral and was consecrated in 1864.

Contact point *Russian Ecclesiastical Mission in Jerusalem (Moscow Patriarchate): tel. 02-625 2565, fax 02-625 6325*

Romanian Orthodox Church

The Romanian Orthodox Church in Jerusalem, St George's, is at 46 Shivtei Israel Street, close to the former Italian hospital and to the Jewish Orthodox quarter outside of the Old City, Mea Shearim. The church is in the same building as the Representation of the Romanian Orthodox Patriarchate at the Holy Places.

St George's is open daily to the public for morning prayers at 7 a.m. and evening prayers at 7 p.m. On Saturdays and Sundays, the Holy Liturgy takes place between 8.30 a.m. and 11 a.m. Memorial services in remembrance of the departed are held after the liturgy on Saturday mornings.

The Festival Day of the church is on St George's Day on 23 April. Other Feast Days and celebrations marked by the Greek Orthodox Patriarchate of Jerusalem are also observed.

The Romanian Church was established in Jerusalem in 1935. Ten years earlier, the Church of Romania, with its headquarters in Bucharest, received the status of Patriarchate in the family of Orthodox churches, recognized as a leading Orthodox Church and Orthodox nation in the world because of its numbers and uninterrupted Christian witness.

Every inch of St George's is covered in frescoes painted by Romanian painters in a neo-Byzantine style. Many of the traditional saints are depicted in vivid colours along the walls of the church. In the entrance hall, or narthex, are many of the Romanian saints and martyrs along with a golden painted map of historical Romania with the Virgin Mary and Christ-Child at its centre. Romanian Orthodox tradition relates that the Virgin Mary asked her son to give her as an earthly dowry the gift of praying and defending the people of a certain land. Christ is said to have given her Mount Athos and the 'ring' of Romania, which is the shape of Romania's map. Thus, Romania is believed to be under her care, with a ring of sanctity drawn around its borders reinforced by the building of many monasteries honouring the Virgin Mary.

During the Saturday memorial service there is a special ceremony involving the blessing and serving of *kollyva*. This is a cake-like dish, made of boiled wheat grains, sugar, spices and ground nuts and sprinkled with icing sugar and coloured sweets. The sign of the cross is etched on the top.

At the end of the service, the dish is held up and then blessed by the priest who says prayers for the departed. It is then distributed to all those present. Being made of wheat which, after burial in the earth, rises to new life, the *kollyva* is a symbol of Resurrection (John 12:24; 1 Cor 15:36, 42–44). The memorial service at which it is distributed is a celebration of life – the new life that awaits Christians in Heaven.

The tradition of serving *kollyva* is common among Christian Orthodox churches. It is particularly associated with the first Saturday of Great Lent when the Great Martyr, St Theodore the Recruit, is remembered. He was a Roman soldier in Asia Minor, martyred in the early fourth century under the Emperor Maximian. According to Church tradition, this saint appeared in a dream to Eudoxius, the Archbishop of Constantinople, and warned him that the Emperor Julian the Apostate (reigned 361–363), as part of his campaign against the Christians, had ordered that the food for sale in the market of the city be sprinkled with blood from pagan sacrifices in order to defile the Christian observance of the first week of Lent. St Theodore ordered Eudoxius to gather the Christian community within the walls of his monastery and only feed them boiled grains of wheat (*kollyva*). In memory of this event, a Prayer of Intercession is sung to St Theodore on the first Saturday of Lent and a dish of *kollyva* is blessed in his honour.

Contact point *Romanian Orthodox Patriarchate's Representation: tel./fax 02-626 4628*

Roman Catholic or Latin Church

The Catholic Church in the Holy Land belongs to seven Catholic Patriarchates: Roman Catholics; Greek Catholics or Melkites; Syrian Catholics; Maronites; Armenian Catholics; Chaldean Catholics; and Coptic Catholics. The two main groups are the Roman Catholics, known in the Holy Land as Latins, and the Greek Catholics. The Latins are the largest group in the city of Jerusalem, with around 5,000 members.

The Latin Patriarchate was established in Jerusalem in 1099 during the Crusades to the Holy Land. A century later, when the Crusaders were conquered and forced to leave the city, the Latin hierarchy fled with them and the Roman Catholic Church lacked local representation. In the absence of a residential Patriarch, Pope Clement VI, in 1342, made the Franciscan friars, led by a *Custos*, the official custodians of the Holy Land. Over the next 500 years, the Franciscans were the Latin Church presence in the Holy Land, guarding the Holy Places and encouraging the growth of the local churches.

In the mid-nineteenth century, the Latin Patriarchate was re-established in Jerusalem, and with its restoration, many other religious orders arrived to serve in the Latin Patriarchal diocese. The chief religious order is still the Franciscan Custody of the Holy Land, drawn from many countries with a special mandate from the Pope to serve the Holy Places, with responsibility today for the majority of biblical sites. In addition to the Franciscans, there are 31 other religious institutes of men and 69 of women. The White Fathers, for example, look after St Anne's Church, the Dominicans, St Stephen's, the Benedictines, the Church of the Dormition, the Sisters of Zion, Ecce Homo, and the Little Sisters of Jesus, the Sixth Station of the Cross.

Latin-rite Catholics are largely Palestinian Arabs with the parish clergy and the Patriarch of Palestinian origin. A helpful starting point to discover more about the Catholic presence in Jerusalem is the Franciscan-run Christian Information Centre at Jaffa Gate in the Old City (see page 125). Check here for the times of all the local church services and for any special Christian events and feast days taking place. It is a good place to buy local maps and guides to the Holy Land. The Franciscans also have a good bookshop, the Franciscan Corner Bookshop, on St Francis Street. Their monastery, St Saviour's, was begun in 1554 and is the biggest monastery in the Holy Land today. The parish church of St Saviour's, also on St Francis Street, is the only Latin Catholic parish church in the Old City.

Here you can join local Christians at worship. There's a daily mass at 7.15 a.m. in Arabic, 8 a.m. in Italian and parish mass on Sunday at 9 a.m., high mass in Arabic at 6 p.m. The Feast of St Francis of Assisi is celebrated on 4 October.

It is from St Saviour's that Franciscans lead pilgrims on the Via Dolorosa every Friday afternoon at 3 p.m. In their sandals and brown robes, the monks walk the Stations of the Cross, following the route it is said Christ took carrying his cross from the Judgement court to Golgotha, the place of the Crucifixion.

The prayers said along the Via Dolorosa are in Italian, Latin and English as the monks pause at each of the fourteen stations for reflection to recall Jesus' suffering. Nine of the stations follow the narrow streets of Jerusalem. The last five are in the Holy Sepulchre where it is believed Christ was crucified, buried and rose again from the dead. Many of the stations are marked by chapels or churches for meditation and prayer. (See the chapter on the Via Dolorosa.)

By special arrangement, pilgrims can organize services in other Catholic churches through the Franciscan Pilgrims' Office at Jaffa Gate. The Cathedral of the Latin Patriarchate in Latin Patriarchate Road, for example, can host 700 people. Here, there's mass at 7 a.m. every day and at 7 a.m. and 9 a.m. on Sundays.

Church of St Peter in Gallicantu

One church recently restored to facilitate large groups of pilgrims
is St Peter in Gallicantu. The panoramic view from the Belvedere
viewpoint on the right before entering the church is worth a few
minutes' stop. Here you overlook the intersection of three valleys
– the Kidron, Tyropoeon and Hinnon (Gehenna) – and get a
bird's eye view of the topography of the ancient city of David.
From here you can imagine the city of Jerusalem at the time of
Jesus and localize many of the events mentioned in the New
Testament.

This church, on the eastern slopes of Mount Zion, can
accommodate a group of 275 pilgrims in one level, 100 in another.
It is open every day except Sunday from 8.30 a.m. to 12 noon and
2 p.m. to 5 p.m. and is run by the Assumptionist Order.

The church's name, literally translated from the Latin, means
'the Church of St Peter at the cock's crow' – commemorating the
events surrounding Jesus' religious trial before Caiaphas and the
Sanhedrin, as well as St Peter's triple denial of Jesus and the
Apostle's subsequent repentance after the cock had crowed.

The church is built over a deep pit which is thought to be
either the cell of the High Priest Caiaphas's palace where Jesus
was kept overnight in solitary confinement after his arrest and
before his trial (Mark 14:53), or where his disciple Peter is said
to have wept bitterly after denying Christ three times (Luke
22:54–62).

There has been a church on this site since the fifth century.
The ancient stepped street on the north side of the church is even
believed to have been in existence at the time of Jesus. This street
once linked the upper city with the lower city and many believe it
is possible Jesus actually walked here. He may, in fact, have taken
this route twice the night before he died – first, when having left
the Upper Room after the Last Supper, he crossed the Kidron
valley on his way to Gethsemane, and second, following his arrest
there, when he returned as a captive to await his religious trial
before Caiaphas. This is perhaps, therefore, one of the most
authentic places for pilgrims wishing to walk where Jesus walked.

Also at the church is a monastic arts and crafts shop which sells handicrafts from approximately 20 monasteries of the Holy Land.

Contact point *Church of St Peter in Gallicantu: tel. 02-673 1739, fax 02-673 4837*

Other members of the Catholic Church family in Jerusalem

Founded by St Maron, the **Maronite Church of Antioch** is the largest Church in Lebanon and is the only Eastern Catholic Church with no Orthodox counterpart. There is a chapel, hostel and the office of the Patriarchal Exarch for Jerusalem and the Holy Land in the Old City near the Jaffa Gate.

The **Chaldean Catholic Church**, separated from the Assyrian Church of the East in the mid-1500s, is now the largest Christian Church in Iraq. Few Chaldeans live in Jerusalem but the Church maintains a presence on Chaldean Street opposite the Ecole Biblique.

Both the **Syrian Catholic Church** and the **Armenian Catholic Church** retain much of the language and liturgy of their Orthodox counterparts but both are in communion with Rome. The Armenians are at the third Station of the Via Dolorosa and the Syrians on Chaldean Street.

Contact points
Latin Patriarchate: tel. 02-628 2323/627 2280, fax 02-627 1652
Franciscans, Fr Emilio Barsena, Christian Information Centre: tel. 02-627 2692, fax 02-628 6417
Syrian Patriarchal Vicariate: tel. 02-628 2657/627 4318, fax 02-628 4217
Maronite Vicariate: tel. 02-628 2158, fax 02-627 2821

Armenian Catholic Patriarchate: tel. 02-628 4262, fax 02-627 2123
Chaldean Patriarchal Vicariate: tel. 02-628 4519

Greek Catholic (Melkite) Church

The Greek Catholic (Melkite) Church was officially founded in 1724 after a split in the Patriarchate of Antioch. One group continued as the Greek Orthodox Church of Antioch with its own Patriarch, while another bishop was recognized by the Roman Pope as the Patriarch of the Greek Catholic Church. Although they have adopted some Roman Catholic practices, the Melkites have maintained the Byzantine liturgy (somewhat abbreviated) and many other Orthodox traditions. Worship is mostly in Arabic.

Today there are 53,000 Greek Catholics in the Holy Land, making them overall the second largest Church after the Greek Orthodox. Around 50,000 live in the Galilee region. There is a small community in Jerusalem centred around the Patriarchate inside Jaffa Gate, a few metres on the left up Greek Catholic Patriarchate Road.

Here, the Greek Catholic Patriarchate church, the Church of the Annunciation, is arguably the most representative Byzantine church in Jerusalem and, ironically, is perhaps the best place to introduce yourself to Orthodox places of worship.

Frescoes of this nineteenth-century church were painted in the mid-1970s by two Romanian brothers, commissioned to use their skill as iconographers in the Holy Land. The result is stunning. Apart from the pillars, the church is almost entirely covered with frescoes. In the Orthodox tradition they are there to draw us into a sacred space out of earthly time and being, into an eternal realm.

The frescoes are painted according to a clear theological plan. Read from the top down and begin at the highest point of the church in the central dome with the fresco of Christ, the

Pantokrator, the Ruler of All, set above all else and the point towards which everything else tends.

Under this, around the dome, is the depiction of the central act of worship, the divine liturgy, and the Twelve Apostles and the major Prophets of the Old Testament. From there the church proceeds in a clockwise plan of decoration depicting the entire life of Christ from the Annunciation to the Resurrection. Each scene is interconnected: take the scene of Christ's birth, painted directly opposite the scene of the Resurrection. Both symbolize why Christ came to earth. In the first icon, Christ is born into a stone coffin, a sarcophagus, a symbol of death. His mother is kneeling next to him, dressed entirely in red. This is unusual: in the East, the Virgin Mary is normally painted in blue and red – the blue standing for heaven, the red for earth – symbolizing the one who combines heaven and earth by giving birth to the God-man. In this scene, however, Mary's dress is explained by looking across the church at the icon of the Resurrection. Here Christ is shown standing on the shattered gates of hell in the form of a cross, bridging the mouth of hell. He is resurrecting out of the sarcophagus Adam and Eve, symbolic of humankind. Eve is dressed in red, just as Mary was, showing that the first Eve, who sinned, is replaced by the second one who gave birth to Christ who overcomes sin and raises us to life.

The second icon therefore completes the scene of the Nativity and explains it theologically. Make the connections from manger to coffin, from swaddling clothes to shroud, from cave to tomb and from birth to death and the new birth of Resurrection.

Learn to read the symbolism. Over the exit of the church, for example, is the scene of the dormition of the Virgin Mary. This is to remind us as we leave the church – this sacred and timeless space – that we are going to return to the world where, inevitably, we are going to die. Mary's death is held up as a model of what our deaths could be: her body lies dead and her soul, in the form of a small baby, is being taken heavenward by Christ. The icon reassures us we will not die alone without protectors and intercessors.

Work your way around the icons, finding out how one scene

interprets another. Read them like a biblical text, cross-referencing and seeing one scene in the context of another. Then work another layer down where, below the scenes of Christ's life, are many icons of saints. They are meant to remind us that when we worship in the Church the saints and the angels are present. The saints are also to remind us of our responsibility to guide others in the path of faith.

Under the lines of saints, at eye level in the church, are painted drawn curtains. Symbolically these may suggest that, at the last day, they will be opened and we will see our own faces glorified.

Try to attend a Divine Liturgy in the church. The worship is in Arabic, with some Greek. Services are on Monday, Tuesday, Wednesday and Friday at 7 a.m., Thursday and Saturday at 6 p.m. and Sunday at 9 a.m.

If you do attend a service of worship, it is helpful to understand the symbolism and function of the icon screen, or iconostasis – one of the most noticeable features of a Byzantine church. In this church, as in all Orthodox churches, the iconostasis divides the nave, the main part of the church, from the sanctuary, where the Holy Sacrifice is offered.

The iconostasis usually has three sets of doors. The one in the centre is called the Royal Door. The Royal Doors open out onto the congregation at three central points in the liturgy: first, when Christ comes in the form of the Gospel, the deacon comes out from the Royal Doors and stands on the steps in front of the doors to read the text; secondly, when the clergy transfer the unconsecrated gifts of bread and wine from the Table of Preparation to the Holy Altar; and thirdly, at the time of Communion when the priest brings out the Chalice containing the Sacrament in order to distribute it to the congregation.

The opening of the Royal Doors is therefore seen to be symbolic of how God erupts into human history – through his Word and his Sacrament. They are the doors from heaven to earth, through which He comes to us and breaks down the barriers of time and space. They also symbolize the stone used to seal the tomb in which Christ was buried and which was moved to reveal the victory over death and the era of God's kingdom.

Again, the icons on each side of the Royal Doors are in
keeping with the Orthodox tradition. Christ is depicted on the
right and the Virgin with the Christ-Child on the left.

Notice how worshippers venerate the icons in the church.
They are venerated, not worshipped, as people prostrate
themselves before them and kiss them. Often people believe
the icons themselves are sacred objects sometimes with miracle-
working powers. People pray in front of them for special gifts of
healing and strength, seeing the icons not as paintings but as
dynamic manifestations of glorified saints who are mystically
present in them.

Candles are used a great deal in Orthodox worship and are
symbolic of the light of Christ. In this church, as in others, you
may see the bishop, priest or deacon in the liturgy carrying in his
right hand a candlestick containing three candles (*trikirion*) and
in his left hand one with two candles (*dikirion*). The three
candles represent the Trinity – three Persons in one God – and
the two represent the two natures of Christ – human and divine –
in one Person. The Byzantine church insists that these doctrines
be proclaimed in word and symbol as they are central to
Christianity.

Greek Melkites cross themselves in the same way as the
Orthodox, head to chest, then from right to left, with thumb and
first two fingers joined in honour of the Trinity. The fourth and
fifth fingers are pressed to the palm, in honour of the two natures
of Christ in one person.

You can join members of the congregation in lighting candles
in front of the iconostasis on special stands to the right and left of
the Royal Doors. Say a prayer as you light your candle.

Greek Melkite Patriarchate Museum

In the hallway near the entrance to the church, still within the
Patriarchal building, is a museum of the different Eastern Church
traditions in the Holy Land. It is worth a brief visit to get a sense
of the colourful diversity of local Christianity. It is open from 9
a.m. to 1 p.m. each day, except Sunday. (If your group calls in

advance, a guide from the church may be able to meet you and explain the museum displays.)

Inside, there is a selection of figures showing the typical religious garb of the different traditions. On the back wall is an altar displaying different objects used in the divine liturgy, such as the *trikirion* and *dikirion*. There are photographs showing scenes of the life of worship in each of the churches and display cases showing such liturgical items as the bread used during the divine liturgy – a round loaf with a square mould imprint in the middle. The square is lifted out and used sacramentally in the Eucharist; the rest is blessed and distributed to the congregation.

Also on display are some of the different crosses and prayer ropes that are distinctive features of worship in the East. You can see them being painstakingly knotted by many of the religious in the different monasteries and constantly in the hand of those praying. At each knot the Jesus prayer is said: 'Lord Jesus Christ, Son of God, have mercy on me.'

Contact point *Greek Catholic (Melkite) Patriarchate: tel. 02-628 2023/627 1968/9, fax 02-628 6652*

The Evangelicals: Anglican and Lutheran Churches

The Jerusalem Dioceses of the Episcopal Church of Jerusalem and the Middle East and the Evangelical Lutheran Church in Jordan share a common inception in the nineteenth-century missionary movement. Their joint Jerusalem bishopric of 1841 lasted 44 years with the break-up seeing England continuing its support of the Anglicans, and Germany, the Lutherans. Today, both churches have Arab bishops and a large number of local schools and social service agencies.

The **Anglican Cathedral** is on Nablus Road in Jerusalem with both an Arab and an expatriate congregation who work closely together. The Cathedral of St George is built in the style of an English cathedral with the nave consecrated in 1898 and the remainder about 1910. During the First World War, the Turks closed the church and used the Bishop's House as their army headquarters. The truce was actually signed in the Bishop's study.

On Sundays there is Holy Communion at 8 a.m. The Eucharist in Arabic is at 9.30 a.m. and in English at 11 a.m. Evensong and Address is at 6 p.m. There is also Holy Communion, Mattins and Evensong every weekday. Peace Prayers take place in St Michael's Chapel in the Cathedral on the first Wednesday of each month at 6.30 p.m.

Within the Cathedral compound is **St George's College**. The College sponsors long- and short-term courses for Christians from around the world, which include field trips and lectures. Around the College is a splendid garden, with identification plaques labelling the trees and plants mentioned in the Bible.

Within the Old City, near the Jaffa Gate, is another Anglican church, **Christ Church**, serving Messianic Jews among its charismatic congregation. In addition to the two Anglican churches in Jerusalem, there are 13 others in Israel, the West Bank and Gaza. The diocese also sponsors a large number of institutions in the fields of education, special education for people with handicaps, pilgrim guest houses and medical care – notably hospitals in Gaza and Nablus.

The **Evangelical Lutheran Church of Jordan (ELCJ)** includes six Arab-speaking congregations in Jerusalem and the West Bank and one in Amman, Jordan. The office of the bishop is located in the Lutheran Church of the Redeemer in the Old City where one of the congregations worships. The ELCJ has a strong educational ministry, with 3,000 pupils in six schools, and is involved in ecumenical work and inter-faith dialogue.

The Church of the Redeemer is owned and operated by the Evangelical Church in Germany and, in addition to the Arab congregation, houses a German-speaking expatriate congregation and an English-speaking expatriate ministry. The Danish Lutherans worship there monthly as well. The church was built in the late nineteenth century on property given to the Prussian king by the Turkish sultan and is modelled after Crusader churches in the Holy Land. The bell tower provides a remarkable overview of the Old City. This is open daily from 9 a.m. to 1 p.m. and 2 p.m. to 5 p.m., and on Fridays from 9 a.m. to 1 p.m.

The German Lutherans established schools, hospices and hospitals in Palestine, including the Hospice of the Order of St John in Jerusalem. Other national Lutheran bodies founded work in the late nineteenth century and the twentieth century, including the Norwegian, Finnish and Swedish Lutherans. Much of the work centres on education and Jewish/Christian relations. The Lutheran World Federation, through ELCJ, supports work including Augusta Victoria Hospital, vocational schools and the Church of the Ascension which services tourists and pilgrims from Germany. Augusta Victoria has no congregation but is used for special services and concerts.

In the twentieth century, and especially since the Second World War, a number of other Protestant groups have started churches. In the Jerusalem area they include: Baptist (Southern); Christian Brethren Assembly; Christian and Missionary Alliance; Church of God; Church of the Nazarene; French Protestant Churches; Jerusalem Bible College; King of Kings Assembly; Korean Presbyterian Church; Netherlands Reformed Church; Scottish Presbyterian Church (St Andrew's); Seventh-day Adventists; St Paul's Pentecostal Fellowship. The Christian Information Centre (see page 125) has information on locations and times of worship.

A growing group of 'churches' that are not Protestant, Orthodox or Catholic are known as Hebrew Christians, Jewish believers or Messianic Jews. Meeting in Messianic assemblies, usually on Saturdays, these groups see themselves as successors of the early Jewish Christians. The Caspari Centre at 36 Jaffa Road (tel. 02-623 3926) can put you in touch with this movement.

Saturday services are held at 3 p.m. in **Christ Church**, across from the Citadel in the Jaffa Gate area. It was the Holy Land's first Protestant church, built by the London Society for Promoting Christianity amongst the Jews (today known as CMJ, the Church's Ministry Among the Jews). Its founders believed that before Jesus returned, the Jewish people would be restored to Israel and that before the end of the age, many Jews would acknowledge Jesus as the Messiah. The church was designed so that Jewish people would enter the building and see the Jewish roots of the Christian faith. Notice the Hebrew script and the Star of David on the altar.

Christ Church today offers pilgrims accommodation and volunteers run a coffee shop and book shop nearby.

Contact points
Anglicans: St George's Cathedral: tel. 02-628 3261, fax 02-627 6401
Lutherans: Lutheran Church of the Redeemer: tel. 02-627 6111, fax 02-628 5764
Christ Church: tel. 02-627 7727/627 7729, fax 02-627 7730

The Holy Sepulchre or the Garden Tomb?

A clash of pieties

The most important stop in any Christian pilgrimage to the Holy Land is at the site of the death, burial and resurrection of Jesus Christ. When Protestant pilgrims come to Jerusalem, that site is the Garden Tomb, a five-minute walk up from Damascus Gate on Nablus Road. On the other hand, with Catholic or Orthodox pilgrims, the tour guide takes them to the Church of the Holy Sepulchre in the midst of the Old City. Some tours might even include both places. But you might well ask, why are there two places? Surely Christ was crucified only once, and laid in only one tomb?

When you visit the two places you will find the contrast quite striking. The Church of the Holy Sepulchre is a busy, noisy, highly decorated space bustling with tourists, full of old columns and rocks, and sometimes music in several languages and keys all at once. The Garden Tomb, in contrast, is a quiet garden with sculpted paths, space for private prayer and a tomb which actually looks like a tomb.

The site of the Holy Sepulchre was identified in AD 326 when Helena, mother of the Roman Emperor Constantine, visited the Holy Land. Although the place was located within the fourth-century city walls by then, Christians of the time were sure of the spot because it was covered by a Roman temple. When the temple was later razed, tombs were found cut into the now exposed hillside. Taking this as proof of the correct place, the Church of the Resurrection was built on the site. The church was completed in AD 348, and also marked the site where Queen

Helena claimed to have found the Cross on which Christ was crucified in an underground cave.

Little remains of that first building, as a result of conquests, earthquakes, fires and rebuilding. It now looks very different! The Greek Orthodox Church, the Armenian Apostolic Church and the Franciscans (Catholic) are the three official custodians of the church, with two Muslim families holding the keys. After a long history of negotiations, a formal 'status quo' for the Church of the Holy Sepulchre, as well as for the other Holy Places, was finalized in 1852. This formal treaty is still valid and includes within its legal ambit the three churches mentioned, in addition to the Syrian, Coptic and Ethiopian Orthodox. It designates such 'rights' as times of worship and processions for each group as well as responsibilities for care, cleaning and renovation.

That this church is on the exact location of the crucifixion and burial has been questioned because the church is inside the present-day city walls and executions and burials took place outside the walls. Most modern archaeologists, however, believe that the place is authentic and that it was indeed outside the city walls in the first-century. Early Christian liturgical celebrations (before AD 66) were held at the site and its memory was kept alive even after Hadrian built a temple on the spot in an effort to obliterate the Christian tradition. There is also clear evidence of a variety of placements for the city walls different from today's sixteenth-century structures.

In 1882 General Gordon, a British soldier and Bible student, saw what appeared to be a human skull on the rock face across from Damascus Gate. Local tradition called it the 'Place of Stoning', which indicated that public executions had taken place there and that the location was outside the city walls. Gordon was convinced that this was the spot, especially since Golgotha (or the 'place of the skull') is mentioned in all four Gospels, and for a time he convinced the Anglican Church to support his claim. A two-chambered tomb has been found on the property, although archaeologists believe that it was made much earlier than the first century AD and would not have been considered a new tomb at the time of Jesus' death. For over 100 years the location has been

owned and cared for by the London-based Garden Tomb Association, formed to keep the site sacred as a quiet spot.
   Visit both!

The Holy Sepulchre

The Holy Sepulchre is open daily from 4 a.m. to 7 p.m. The Christian Information Centre (page 125) at Jaffa Gate has the times of the services of the various communities.

The best time to visit the Holy Sepulchre is early Sunday morning between 6 a.m. and 8.30 a.m. Then the church is a place of worship rather than a noisy, bustling museum for large tour groups. Many of the local Christian churches hold their services here on Sunday mornings – often at the same time. On entering, you are greeted by what sounds like a twentieth-century Pentecost, a medley of different languages and liturgies unfamiliar to a Western ear. At best, this can be a mystical and spiritual experience in the quiet of early morning when Jerusalem is waking up to the bells of its churches.

If you are there early enough you can see the daily solemn ritual of the church being opened. Since shortly after the end of the Crusades, two Muslim families have had control of the door of the church. One holds the key; the other has the right to open it. Each morning, one of the communities with 'rights' in the church knocks at the wicket. A Greek sacristan calls the Muslim doorkeeper and hands him out a ladder, which is used to reach the door lock. Three bells announce the opening, one for each of the three 'major' communities – Greek Orthodox, Armenian Orthodox and Catholic – all of whom must agree that the church is opened.

Once inside the church, join the Syrians at 8.30 a.m. (one hour later in summer) in the oldest section of the building, the Syrian Orthodox chapel of St Nicodemus. Here the liturgy is robustly chanted in Aramaic, the language of Christ.

On the left are two small burial chambers known as the tombs of Joseph of Arimathea and of Nicodemus, dating from the first century, which have been taken to indicate that this area of Jerusalem at that time was outside the city walls and was being used as a burial place. Burials never took place within the city confines as the ground was thus rendered unclean.

Close by, and almost, it seems, in competition, the Greek Orthodox chant their liturgy. Join the Armenians at 8.45 a.m. or the Catholics at 7 a.m. (8 a.m. in the summer).

Sunday morning liturgies at the Tomb of the Holy Sepulchre itself are Coptic at 4 a.m., Latin at 5.30 a.m., Greek at 7 a.m., Syrian at 8 a.m. and, on alternating Sundays, Armenian at 8.45 a.m.

This is a wonderful way to see and hear many of the churches gathered together and worshipping God in their distinctive traditions. For all the well-known divisions and quarrels of the churches of Jerusalem over this holy site, where else in the world would you get such a marketplace of Christian traditions actually worshipping under the same roof – Catholic with Eastern Orthodox with Oriental Orthodox?

Other good times to visit are early morning or early evening when the tour groups ebb or Friday afternoon from 3.30 p.m. joining the last of the Franciscan Stations of the Cross on the Via Dolorosa or the 4 p.m. Latin procession around the church to sing Vespers. Armenians have their procession around the church every Friday and Saturday at 4.15 p.m. (5.15 p.m. summertime).

One of the quietest places in the church to meditate can be the twelfth-century Armenian Crypt of St Helena. The walls on either side of the steps leading down to the Crypt are covered with crosses etched by medieval pilgrims. From here thirteen narrow steps, in the right hand corner, lead down to an area reputed to be where St Helena discovered the Cross on which Christ was crucified.

Back in the main body of the church, notice the newly decorated rotunda over the Tomb of Christ. Plans to restore and repair the dome began in 1959. Agreement was finally achieved between the three custodians of the church and the new dome was dedicated in 1997.

The design embodies common attributes of the three communities and represents the glory of God enveloping the Risen Christ. It consists of twelve streams of gold, representing the Twelve Apostles. From each ray branch three streams of light symbolizing the Father, the Son and the Holy Spirit. Light from the dome's central skylight, as well as from concealed artificial sources, enhances the mother-of-pearl background which brightens as it ascends and sparkles with stars. The background is a representation of the biblical description of the luminous cloud of the Presence of God.

The decorations, like the angels that spoke in the garden to the women who were shocked by the empty tomb, are meant to lift our eyes heavenwards saying: 'Why do you seek the living among the dead?' (Luke 24:5). 'He is risen' (Matthew 28:6).

Symbolically the decoration is also meant to represent the goodwill and love among the current custodians. It is seen as a sign of a new era of co-operation among the churches in Jerusalem.

The new dome of the Holy Sepulchre was financed by one of the Knights of the Holy Sepulchre. The members of this ancient order are the inheritors of the Knights of Crusader times, formed by Godfrey de Bouillon in the eleventh century to guard the Holy Sepulchre after Jerusalem had been wrested from Muslim control. De Bouillon's sword and spurs can be seen today in the sacristy of the church.

Today's Knights hold some services of investiture and procession in the Church. On their investiture they are given a long cloak with a huge scarlet cross of Jerusalem on the left hand side, spurs and a sword. The spurs and sword are only used at the time of investiture and are not part of the processional regalia.

Today, they are an international body with 43 lieutenancies, mainly in Europe and North America. Knights and Dames are invited to join the order, which is under the patronage of the Pope. They undertake to make regular pilgrimages to the Holy Land and finance all of the work of the Latin Patriarchate of Jerusalem, which includes about 60 parishes, 40 schools and a thriving seminary.

There are 18,000 Knights and Dames worldwide. Their services, while on pilgrimage, include a solemn entry into the Church of the Holy Sepulchre, dressed in full regalia, and are worth watching out for.

For a detailed guide to the Holy Sepulchre, read *The Holy Sepulchre: The Church of the Resurrection – An Ecumenical Guide* by J. Robert Wright, published by the Ecumenical Theological Research Fraternity in Israel.

The Garden Tomb

The Garden Tomb is open Monday to Saturday from 8.30 a.m. to 12 noon and from 2 p.m. to 5.30 p.m. It is closed on Sundays except for a service in English at 9 a.m.

Easter Day is obviously a special day in the Garden Tomb. Many pilgrims find that worshipping with the empty tomb as a visual aid can help re-live the experience of Jesus' followers at the Crucifixion and their joy at the Resurrection. Every Easter Sunday hundreds of people come to the Garden, starting before dawn for successive services in six different languages until midday. Services are in German, English, Scandinavian languages, Finnish, Dutch and French. There is also a sunrise service in Arabic on Orthodox Easter Sunday at 6.30 a.m.

The Garden Tomb can be booked in advance for groups wanting to hold their own services of worship. Book at least a few months in advance to guarantee a space. The central platform area for seated worship can hold groups of up to 150 people. This can be a powerfully symbolic and quiet place to reflect on the last days of Christ's life, his death and Resurrection and to share the Eucharist together.

This is also one of the few places of planted greenery in East Jerusalem where it is possible to sit and reflect and escape from the noise of Jerusalem or the heat of the day. In the Resurrection Garden there are many quiet secluded places to sit if you come on your own. There is also a prayer room for reflection and meditation.

Contact point *Tel. 02-627 2745, fax 02-627 2742*

A walk down the Mount of Olives

The Mount of Olives is the location of many events in the week before Christ's crucifixion: the route of his triumphal entry into Jerusalem before the Passover started from here; his arrest in the Garden of Gethsemane took place here and the place of his Ascension is believed to be at the top of the central peak. It is also where Jesus came to sleep, to pray and to visit friends at Bethany, the village on the Mount of Olives in which Jesus' friends Martha, Mary and Lazarus lived. From its cemetery Jesus raised Lazarus from the dead.

On Palm Sunday in the Western calendar (see pages 112–15), join the Franciscans, local Christians and pilgrims who walk from the Latin church at Bethphage (the site mentioned in Mark 11:1 as the beginning of Jesus' procession into Jerusalem) down the Mount of Olives. (See the chapter on Christian celebrations on page 115.) Otherwise, make the walk yourself, stopping at some of the key locations for a moment's reflection and quiet prayer.

Wear sensible shoes – the path is steep and slippery. Except for Palm Sunday, don't go on a Sunday – many of the sites are closed. Women are advised to go as part of a group rather than on their own.

Start at the top of the Mount of Olives, close to the village of A-Tur, at the **Chapel of the Ascension of Christ.** It is marked by a small minaret and a mosque, as the site is today under Muslim control. This is the traditional site of the Ascension of Jesus 40 days after the Resurrection (Luke 24:50–52). The New Testament tells how Jesus was lifted up and hidden by a cloud as he blessed the disciples. Here, in the small octagonal shrine, an indentation in the stone is believed to be the right footprint of Jesus as he left this earth. In the early thirteenth century, the building underwent reconstruction and the left footprint of Jesus was removed to Al-Aqsa mosque.

Notice the metal rings set into the walls from which the various local Christian communities stretch awnings to provide a temporary roof for the annual celebration of the Feast of the Ascension.

Meditate

Here is the footprint of Jesus on earth.
How is Jesus visible among us today?
Do we recognize him around us?

About 25 metres south of the Chapel of the Ascension, on the left, is the **Church of the Paternoster** and the **Grotto of the Paternoster.**

Visit the grotto first. This is the place tradition says Jesus taught his disciples the Lord's Prayer (Luke 11:2–4) and preached on the ultimate conflict of good and evil leading to the end of the world (Matthew 24:1–25).

The grotto had been identified by the third century and was visited by early pilgrims. However, a cloister was built on the site in 1868 by Aurella, Princess de la Tour d'Auvergne, who bought the property and built the adjoining convent of contemplative Carmelite sisters to ensure the grotto would always be surrounded by veneration and prayer.

The inner walls of the cloister commemorate the teaching of the Lord's Prayer, with the prayer inscribed in over 70 languages on colourful ceramic tiles.

It is open daily, except Sunday, from 8.30 to 11.45 p.m. and 3 p.m. to 4.45 p.m.

Meditate

Say the Lord's Prayer aloud in your own language. Reflect on the prayer itself and on the time devoted to prayer in your life.

From the Paternoster follow a steep lane down towards

Gethsemane. On the right is the entrance to the Franciscan church of **Dominus Flevit.**

Here on the western slopes of the Mount of Olives, Jesus wept over Jerusalem as he rode towards it on Palm Sunday (Luke 19:41–44; Matthew 23:37–39). The present church was built in the shape of a teardrop in 1955 on the ruins of an ancient church.

Today the arched wrought-iron grille window above the altar frames the view of the city over which Jesus wept.

Meditate

Reflect on Jerusalem today – a city of suffering and strife for people of all faiths. Pray that it might become a city of peace and that the tears of those who live within its walls today may cease.

Further down the lane is the **Garden of Gethsemane** and the **Church of All Nations.**

The word Gethsemane is a Greek word from the Hebrew *gat shemen*, meaning 'oil press' or 'oilstores'. In the garden there are eight ancient and gnarled olive trees – held by tradition to be the silent witnesses of Jesus' prayer and suffering the evening before his crucifixion (Matthew 26:36). The rock on which Jesus is supposed to have sat while he prayed is enclosed in the adjoining Church of All Nations, also called the Church of the Agony. Here Jesus faced his impending death knowing his life to be in danger (John 11:8, 16) and suspecting Judas of treachery (Mark 14:17–21). Here he struggled with whether to escape or face his arrest and death.

A church was first built here in the fourth century; the present church was built by the Franciscans in 1924, financed by twelve different countries.

The golden mosaic of its facade depicts Jesus assuming the suffering of the world. Inside, the rock of the agony is directly in front of the altar. The iron wreath, partially enclosing the rock, represents the crown of thorns. The natural light is dimmed by the purple glass in the side windows. This is the 'hour when darkness reigns' of Luke 22:53 and a time for prayer.

Meditate

Reflect on the suffering Jesus knew was ahead of him on the Cross and on his willingness to accept that suffering for our sake. What should our response be to such suffering? Are we prepared to suffer for the sake of others?

Descend to the main road and turn right. Almost hidden in the valley is the **Tomb of the Virgin Mary** or the **Church of the Assumption.** It is open from 6 a.m. to 11 a.m. and 2 p.m. to 5 p.m. and closed on Sundays.

To the right of the entrance to the Tomb is a passage leading to the **Cave of Gethsemane** or the **Grotto of the Agony.**

This grotto is said to be the location of the place where the disciples slept while Jesus prayed in his Agony. Also here, Jesus is believed to have been betrayed by Judas Iscariot and arrested (Luke 22:39; John 18:1; Matthew 26:49; Luke 22:47–48). Here Jesus was bound and lead away to his religious trial, prior to his crucifixion (Luke 22:54; John 18:12–13).

This, it seems, was a place Jesus knew well. St Luke tells us in 21:37 that in his last days Jesus spent the nights on the Mount of Olives, either seeking hospitality among his friends in Bethany or stopping at the foot of the mountain in the place called Gethsemane. St John says Judas knew the place well as Jesus often met his disciples there.

Meditate

Reflect on our inability today to be vigilant or loyal in Jesus' service – either in prayer, priority or in solidarity with others who are suffering. Are we constantly too tired, too preoccupied with our own lives and concerns? Are there actions in our own lives today which have betrayed others as Jesus was betrayed?

Return to the courtyard at the entrance to the Grotto. Descend the wide staircase into the **Tomb of the Virgin Mary,** also known as the **Church of the Assumption.**

About halfway down the steps to the lower storey of the

Byzantine church on the right, Mary's parents, St Joachim and St Anne, are said to be buried. On the left is the tomb of Joseph, Mary's husband. The stone tomb of Mary is in a small square chapel in the lower church, with a rock bench on which her body is said to have been laid.

The church is now used by the Eastern Orthodox Churches. There is also a prayer niche, or *mihrab*, for Muslim worship as Muslims revere Mary as the Mother of the Prophet Jesus.

Orthodox Christians annually celebrate the Feast of the Assumption here on 28 August (see the chapter on Christian celebrations on page 117).

Traditions about the death of Mary in Jerusalem, her burial and her assumption date back to the second and third centuries. That she was 'assumed into heaven' was proclaimed as a doctrine of the Roman Catholic Church in 1950. The belief, however, is much older. The Feast of the Assumption on 15 August was made a public holiday in England by King Alfred the Great; he believed that she is as we may hope to be.

Meditate

In this quiet place, away from the main tourist sites of the Mount of Olives, reflect on your own future when you die and what you believe, or hope, might happen. Do the events in the Garden of Gethsemane or in the Grotto of the Agony and then on the Cross, make any real difference to your thoughts?

This is a quiet space to sit, light a candle and draw strength from the events of Holy Week, to move from Palm Sunday to Easter Day and on to our own Resurrection with the Risen Christ.

Via Dolorosa

This is a journey along the Via Dolorosa to introduce you to some local Christians and their church leaders in Jerusalem today. With the addition of some prayers at various Stations, this journey was undertaken by Alison Hilliard for broadcast on the BBC World Service during Holy Week 1997, and this chapter is transcribed from that broadcast.

It follows the route used by the Franciscan monks at 3 p.m. every Friday afternoon, stopping at some of the fourteen Stations of the Cross along the Via Dolorosa, or the Sorrowful Way. Since the sixteenth century, Via Dolorosa has been the name given to the devotional walk through the streets of Jerusalem that retraces the route followed by Jesus as he carried his cross to Golgotha.

The First Station

Here Jesus is condemned to death.

> *Pilate protested 'What crime has he committed?' They only shouted the louder 'Crucify him, crucify him.' So Pilate, who wished to satisfy the crowd, released Barabbas to them and after he had had Jesus scourged he handed him over to be crucified.*
>
> (Mark 15:14–15)

Today the site of the first station is a busy place where traders and donkeys weave their way through the traffic, the tourists and the shopkeepers. A few steps in one direction there is a Muslim Palestinian school. A few steps in the other, armed Israeli soldiers guard the exit point of the controversial underground tunnel which leads to the Western Wall. Its opening in 1996 sparked clashes between Israeli security forces and Palestinians, leaving scores of people dead and injured.

Our guide to the first station is Bishop Samir Kafity, the Anglican Bishop in Jerusalem (retired September 1998):

'We are standing at the first station, on the road to life – a road which starts with death. This is where Jesus was condemned to death and where Jesus was brought to court. This is where the people who received him and welcomed him on Palm Sunday, shouted "Crucify him, Crucify him". This is the place where Jesus was beaten and mocked at. This is the beginning of the paradox of life, the beginning of the fourteen Stations of the Cross.

'As a Jerusalemite, a native Palestinian Christian, I can imagine, even today, seeing Jesus being condemned to death from the beginning of this road. I can still see the paradox of life and death. I can still see the paradox of playing with justice and with human rights. I can see much recurring that was happening at the time of the first journey of the cross.

'You are now in a place which is holy not because we want to call it holy, but because God himself made his journey into history through these places. It is to me a very vivid place. The new life began here with the sentencing to death of our Lord Jesus Christ.'

The Second Station

Here Jesus takes up the Cross.

Then the soldiers led him into the courtyard of the palace, that is the Governor's headquarters, and they called together the whole cohort. And they clothed him in a purple cloak. And after twisting some thorns into a crown, they put it on him. They struck his head with a reed, spat upon him and knelt down in homage to him. After mocking him, they stripped him of the purple cloak and put his own clothes on him. Then they led him out to crucify him, and carrying the Cross by himself, Jesus went out to what is called the place of the skull.

(Mark 15:16–17, 19–20; John 19:17)

The Reverend Naim Ateek is the Director of the Sabeel
Liberation Theology Centre in Jerusalem, an ecumenical centre
which works with the Christian communities in the city. What
does the second Station of the Cross mean to him today?

'To begin with one needs to remember the way the Romans
tortured people was very terrible. People who were condemned to
death were subjected to all forms of physical as well as
psychological torture. And so, the first thing that comes to
mind, when I reflect on what happened to Jesus, is the way many
people today are still tortured by people in power. Unfortunately,
in many places in the world, including our own country in Israel
and Palestine, it seems that nothing has changed, that many
prisoners and detainees are subject to great torture. And so, I
think of Jesus, the one who has been tortured, standing today in
solidarity with all those who undergo torture, and all kinds of
indignities in the prisons of our modern world.

'Beyond that, as happened with Jesus, after he was tortured, he
was asked to carry his cross. And so Jesus walked through
Jerusalem's streets to the place where he was crucified outside the
city walls. This is also very important for us as we reflect on it.
There are people who have carried crosses, their own crosses, as a
punishment for crimes which they have done. But there are other
crosses, which many innocent people carry on behalf of others,
especially those who carry crosses as they stand for justice and
suffer for it in order to bring liberation to other people. Jesus, I
believe, carried his cross willingly. He wanted to bring salvation to
others. And, by doing so, Jesus forever transformed the cross
from a symbol of shame and guilt to a symbol of outgoing love.
Whenever then we bear the cross of pain and shame willingly, in
order to contribute to the doing of justice for others, I believe we
are walking with Jesus and in the spirit of Jesus. And we, like
Jesus, transform the cross into a symbol of sacrificial love.

'Having said that, I also believe that Jesus today still carries the
cross on behalf of many oppressed people in the world – people
who are subjected to unjust structures, to a life under occupation,
as the Palestinian community is, to a life of dehumanization and
humiliation. I believe Jesus still carries the cross on behalf of
millions of people and he calls us to join him through the many
Via Dolorosas of the world.'

The Third Station

Here Jesus fell for the first time under the weight of the Cross.

The Fourth Station

The Armenian Catholic Church of Our Lady of the Spasm commemorates the fourth Station where Mary stood and watched her son go by. Inside you can see the outline of a pair of sandals, said to be Mary's footprints, on the remarkable fifth-century mosaic floor.

Dr Harry Hagopian is an Armenian Jerusalemite and Executive Director of the Middle East Council of Churches' Jerusalem Liaison Office:

> 'O God, as we pause at this station, we remember the anguish of Jesus' mother watching her son struggle under the burden of the cross. We can almost sense the overwhelming grief which must have gripped her soul and bent her in sorrow. We also feel her powerlessness against the forces set against her son, wondering whether she should plead with You to take away this suffering from the child she had borne.
>
> 'Here, O Lord, we recall all mothers and fathers who are still forced to watch the daily suffering of their children, who see them being handed over to death. We bow down before You in contrition because we often fail to stand up against such agony, allowing the forces of death and destruction to continue to hold sway in our world. Renew our strength, Father, that we, like Mary, might rush to the side of those who shoulder the cross today. Equip us to stand boldly beside those who are crushed by these principalities and powers and to labour for love, compassion, justice and mercy, seeking to end the ways of violence.
>
> 'In Jesus' name, we pray. Amen.'

The Fifth Station

Here the Cyrenean helps Jesus carry the cross.

As they led him away, they laid hold of one Simon, from Cyrene,
who was coming in from the fields. They put the cross on Simon's
shoulder for him to carry along behind Jesus.

(Luke 23:26)

Simon of Cyrene was not from Jerusalem; he is thought to have
been a native of the northern coast of Africa. That is of
significance for Monsignor Michel Sabbah, the Latin Patriarch of
Jerusalem:

'I think here of the universality of Jerusalem and of the
universality of the mystery of Salvation represented by Jesus and
done by Jesus himself. Simon of Cyrene was a foreigner but he
was living in Jerusalem, he was coming to Jerusalem for some
reason connected with the religious character and mystery of
Jerusalem. We live always this mystery of Jerusalem, which
belongs to its own sons and daughters, but which also belongs to
all humankind. If you meditate upon the mystery of Jerusalem, it
is not only the city, it is Jesus and what Jesus has done in this city
to offer salvation to all humankind without any discrimination –
to Jews, Christians and Muslims – to those who accepted and
believed in him and those who did not and do not, until now,
know him and accept him. The fact that Simon, a foreigner,
helped Jesus carry his cross points us again to the mystery of Jesus
in his own land. He was rejected. The Gospel of St John, chapter
one, says he came to his home and he was rejected by his family
and by his own people. That an outsider therefore comes and
bears the cross for him is another sign that Jesus is not only for his
own people, he is for all the world, for everyone. There is no
outsider, or insider for Jesus. All of us are insiders. We are the one
family of God without any limits of nationality, religion or creed.'

The Sixth Station

Here Veronica wipes the face of Jesus.

There was in him no stately bearing to make us look at him, no
appearance that would attract us to him. He was spurned and
avoided by men, a man of suffering, accustomed to infirmity, one

*of those from whom men hide their faces, spurned and we held him
in no esteem.*

(Isaiah 53:2–3)

Who could recognize in the face of Jesus, drawn and haggard,
coated with the dust of the road and streaked with blood and
sweat, the face of a dying man, the true image of God. Everytime
we see his face in the face of one of his suffering little ones we are
privileged to see God face to face.

St George's Cathedral, *The Way of the Cross in Jerusalem*

The story of Veronica has no basis in Scripture. The fourteenth-
century account, however, has Veronica on her way to market,
taking pity on Jesus as he struggled under his cross. She used her
veil to wipe the perspiration from his face and, so the legend goes,
when she took the veil back, the face of Jesus was imprinted on it.
Veronica's gratuitous act of love at this station catches the very
heart of God – according to Lynda Brayer, a Jew who became a
Catholic in the 1980s.

Today Lynda Brayer is the executive legal director of the
Society of St Yves, a Jerusalem-based Catholic legal resource
centre which, for example, provides legal help to Palestinians who
have been arrested or imprisoned, who have had their land
confiscated or house demolished or who have become refugees. It
is in such work that Lynda Brayer remembers the Sixth Station
and hears Veronica's call to action and compassion:

'I think it is a station for every man and every woman. I think it
poses to us the question of what would we have done had we
been standing there? How would we have reacted to have seen
this man who had been beaten, who was being taunted, who was
being led to his death? Where would we have put ourselves?
Would we have had the courage, the compassion to go towards
him, to take a cloth, to wipe his face? I don't know. I think, in
one sense, it is almost a summing up of Thomas à Kempis's idea
of *Imitatio Dei* – in other words, what Veronica did for him, we
are challenged to do for the least of our brothers. We were not at
the cross. We were not at the walk towards Golgotha, but we are
in our everyday lives confronted with the least of our brothers,

with those who are rejected, those who are oppressed – particularly in my work. I think, therefore, that I am personally called to answer the question, am I prepared to wipe the face of the least of my brothers? And if Jesus is the least of my brothers, am I really prepared to wipe his face?

'I think the image of Veronica is: what would I, or anybody, spontaneously do if we saw another person suffering? There is no record of anybody else making a physical move towards this man. Within the context of Jewish law, Veronica might have been breaking the prohibition of purity laws. She obviously was taking a huge risk in going forward to someone who had already been rejected by the religious establishment and by the crowd who followed the religious establishment. She might even have been endangering her life. But, on the other hand, this legend is the only event which tells us of somebody taking themselves and their body and going up to Jesus and wiping his face and trying to physically help him.

'In one sense when we are exhorted to come to Jesus as little children, I think it is also a call to us to stop thinking so much about what we are going to do – to just go out and do the right thing and stop justifying ourselves for not taking action.

'Veronica's name means the true image, and this is how we are called upon to behave – to wipe the face of the poor and everyone who needs it.'

The Seventh Station

The place of Jesus' second fall.

The Eighth Station

Here Jesus meets the Holy Women of Jerusalem.

A great crowd of people followed him, including women who beat their breasts and lamented over him. Jesus turned to them and said 'Daughters of Jerusalem, do not weep for me, weep for yourselves and for your children. For if they do this when the wood is green, what will happen when it is dry?'

(Luke 23:27–28, 31)

The Eighth Station has a particular poignancy for Samia Khoury, a Catholic Jerusalemite and former President of the Young Women's Christian Association – the YWCA – of Palestine:

'I feel distressed because the weeping has not stopped and the women of Jerusalem, whether Jewish, Christian or Muslim, have had their share of weeping. But, for me, as a Palestinian Christian, the weeping still goes on, because the suffering and dispossession has not stopped. So I feel very sad about how right Jesus was even after 2,000 years. These women were not crying for him, they were crying for themselves and their children and their grandchildren.

'I too have had my share of crying. I think every Palestinian who has lived in Jerusalem has had her share of crying. I went through hard times when my son was taken to jail because he had made music, naturally expressing his feelings as an artist about all the injustice of the long years of occupation. I cried because my brother was picked up one evening and thrown over the borders simply because he was a symbol of leadership. And I had a cousin who was also executed in a hit squad in Lebanon. But, surprisingly, I am not bitter.

'I am not bitter because I feel my faith has helped me and so many of us, to be able to survive. It has sustained us all during these difficult times because we believe in a God of love and justice and if we truly believe that, eventually we will overcome. That is why it does not help if you are bitter. In fact, it gives you more hope if you are not bitter and you keep going, working and doing what is right and you believe eventually that justice and peace will prevail. When you have been through the Crucifixion and all the suffering of Holy Week, then it is climaxed by the Resurrection. This alone gives you hope that no suffering will continue for eternity and that there is bound to be a Resurrection and an end to weeping.

'It is true that all women in this city have suffered, women of all faiths, for different reasons. Because Jerusalem has seen so much suffering, so many wars, we feel we relate to each other in the suffering as women. Many times you would find women from various faiths getting together for the sake of the next generation trying to put an end to all the suffering, so that we will have a truly holy Jerusalem where all people can live in peace in this city of peace.

'We pray for all women everywhere, especially those who weep and especially for the women of Jerusalem today. We pray for each time right is obscured by might and the weak and the poor are marginalized and we pray for ourselves that we may have the mind of Christ to love and respect all God's children.'

The Ninth Station

This Station is up a flight of 28 stone steps that leads to the Coptic Patriarchate. A Roman pillar here marks Jesus' third fall.

The Coptic Orthodox Metropolitan of Jerusalem and the Near East, Dr Anba Abraham, reflects, in prayer, on Jesus falling three times under the weight of the Cross:

'Here at this place, oh Lord, my God, I feel ashamed of my sins and those of humanity which You had to bear on the cross. You willingly, Lord, bore those heavy burdens for me, even though it made You fall under the Cross in order to remove the yoke of my sins. Your unlimited humbleness makes me wonder! You agreed to unite with our human nature, in order to annihilate the death of sin and instead give us eternal life. You have hidden away from Satan the Power and Glory of Your Divinity by falling under the Cross as if You were weak, while instead You are the source of all power.

'My heart is deeply stirred when I stand here and remember the agony and pain You went through for my sake, the great love which made You bear all this. Truly, "Greater love hath no man than this, that a man lay down his life for his friends" (John 15:13).'

The last five Stations of the Cross are all located inside the Church of the Holy Sepulchre, which is thought by today's biblical scholars to be the actual site of Christ's Crucifixion, death, burial and Resurrection.

To reach Calvary, where Christ was crucified, climb one of the two steep stairways immediately inside the door of the Holy Sepulchre. At the top of the steps are two altars and a silver disc with a hole which marks the exact spot where the cross on which Christ was crucified was hammered into the rock of Golgotha.

The Tenth Station

Here Jesus is stripped of his clothes.

The Eleventh Station

Here Jesus is nailed to the cross.

They crucified him and the criminals as well – one on his right and the other on his left. Jesus said 'Father forgive them, they do not know what they are doing.'

(Luke 23:33–34)

At the eleventh Station, it is traditional for pilgrims to meditate on the meaning of forgiveness. Archbishop Torkom Manoogian, the Armenian Patriarch of Jerusalem, believes the example set here by Jesus is one of the most challenging messages of the Christian faith:

'The Eleventh Station is about pain and forgiveness – two issues as powerful in our lives today as at the time Christ was crucified. Crucifixion was a painfully brutal death and at this station we are reminded of what Jesus had to physically suffer. Christ's response to his pain is to say "Father forgive them, they do not know what they are doing".

'Wrestling with the issue of forgiveness can be one of the most painful and difficult dilemmas we face as Christians. What example does Christ set for his followers? I'm often asked how can we Armenians forgive those who massacred one and a half million of our people in 1915? What then do Jesus' words at the Eleventh Station have to say to us as a people and to other peoples who have suffered genocide?

'Those who killed Armenians in 1915 and before knew what they were doing. The hangings, starvations, drownings and shootings were all deliberate acts. But how many were truly aware that they were killing someone made in the image of God? Did they know that all human life is sacred in the sight of the creator God? Were they aware of the future consequences of destroying such sacred life? Or had the Armenians merely become the outsider, the enemy, the other, who was without value – despised and dispensable?

'Forgiveness, however, is not mine to grant. That power lies only with a God who is all-knowing. We can ask God to forgive those who have caused us suffering and leave the process of forgiveness to the justice of God. We should also remember that asking God to forgive our enemy does not mean that we need to forget. Forgiving and forgetting are not the same. Forgiving does not mean that we give up preaching that taking the life of someone because he is of a different race or creed or colour is wrong and that all life is sacred. Christ's crucifixion must be our example. We know how easy it is to get carried away with the tide of public feeling. In our hearts we know too that we could have been that executioner or in the crowd crying "Crucify, crucify Him!". We need to be thankful that Christ, in the midst of his suffering, taught us to say "Father, forgive them, they do not know what they are doing".'

The Twelfth Station

Here Jesus dies on the cross.

Jesus uttered a loud cry and said 'Father, into your hands I commend my spirit'. After he said this, he expired.
(Luke 23:46)

The Twelfth Station in the Church of the Holy Sepulchre is cared for by the Greek Orthodox Church. Above the ornate altar, with its candles and its lamps, hangs an image of the crucified Christ – his arms outstretched, his side pierced. Tens of thousands of pilgrims come here each year to pray at the very stone which held the cross on which Christ died. It is a special place too for Metropolitan Timotheus, the Secretary-General of the Greek Orthodox Patriarchate in Jerusalem.

'Every pilgrim kneels in order to venerate this hole and many pilgrims put their hands inside to touch the actual rock. This area around the altar was uncovered lately by the Greek Orthodox Patriarchate in order to give the real picture of the rock to the visitor. Here the bare rock of Calvary is exposed and you can also see the crack which is dated from the very day of the Crucifixion as described in the Gospels.

'It says that the moment the Lord gave up his spirit the rocks were cracked and the tombs opened and the dead people arose and walked and many of their relatives saw them and even talked with them. So this crack is confirmation of what the Gospels say and that this is the real place where the Crucifixion took place.

'This site of Calvary is not only my life – but my life is nothing without this place.

'Calvary gives life to all human beings because the Crucifixion, the ultimate sacrifice, was made for all – for those who were before and those who are living today and those who will be in the generations to come. When I come here, I feel closer to God, closer to the pain that he felt for me and for my sins, and I feel the pain of all those people who are unjustly suffering and I believe that it is my duty to associate myself with all of them and ask my Lord, who suffered unjustly, to alleviate their sufferings. As a hymn of our Church says, he extended his hands in order to bring together the divided, to bring together the human being with Almighty God, God the Father. He is teaching us from the Cross, even silently – forgive, reconcile.'

The Thirteenth Station

Here Jesus' body is removed from the Cross.

The Fourteenth Station

Here Jesus is laid in the tomb.

In the place where he had been crucified, there was a garden and in the garden, a new tomb in which no-one had ever been buried. Because of the Jewish preparation day, they buried Jesus there, for the tomb was close at hand.

(John 19:41–42)

The last Station of the Cross on the Via Dolorosa is at the site of the empty tomb in the Holy Sepulchre. The tomb today is the

central focus of the whole church. Above it, the roof has been
newly decorated with stars and golden rays and sparkling mother-
of-pearl. It is a dramatic backdrop for Christianity's most
important site. The Anglican Bishop in Jerusalem, Bishop Samir
Kafity, who began this journey with us, is again our guide:

'We are at the empty tomb, where Jesus Christ came back to life
after being condemned to death. This is the place where the new
beginning, the new life, the New Testament, was started. There
are people from every nation coming to pay homage and to pray
and worship the living Lord here. There are many Cathedrals in
the world with full tombs. This is the only Cathedral in the world,
the Cathedral of Jerusalem, which has an empty tomb. I am
always reminded when I come here as a native of this city of
Jerusalem, at the end of fourteen Stations of pain and suffering,
that the mixture of pain and glory ends up here – glory starts
from this place. I am delighted to say that we have a new greeting
which comes out this place – the greeting "Christ is risen
indeed!". It is a greeting of life. I am reminded of St John who
quoted Jesus saying "I came that you might have life and have it
abundantly". We are having this life from this empty tomb.

'Going through to the inner chamber to the site of the empty
tomb itself, we enter into the innermost of life, the innermost of
Christianity, the innermost of this Cathedral, which is the empty
tomb. There is no corpse here. Christ is living and you can see
people worshipping here from all over the world. We are at the
holiest of the holies. We are at the heart of the Christian faith.
This is where our Via Dolorosa comes not to an end but to a
beginning, a beginning from the tomb of life, where my Lord has
risen and your Lord is risen that the world may believe and may
become a better world where people of all nations, who are made
of one blood, become one family throughout the world.'

A Holy Week walk

The Via Dolorosa is a Western devotion, observed especially by Latin Catholics. Over the years the specific stops have changed and several non-biblical stations have been introduced. For some Christians there is interest in visiting the actual places of Jesus' last days including the events of the arrest and condemnation. Many of the locations in this route were considered to be the correct location of events in the early church and by the fourth century they were regularly visited for liturgies on Holy Days.

Here then is a Holy Week Walk which begins with the Upper Room, site of the Last Supper, and visits places thought to be equally sacred as the Stations of the traditional Via Dolorosa. Because of the distance across the Kidron valley, you may wish to begin at Gethsemane, Location 2, having visited the Upper Room at another time.

The walk is based on the narrative in St Luke but other Gospel alternatives are also offered. The resources for each location include scriptures, a paragraph about the place itself, a suggested piece of music, and a word to ponder. If your group is familiar with another appropriate piece of music, feel free to make substitutions. If they don't know the music printed here (on pages 130–2), take time for practice in advance. You may use the 'word' to encourage thoughts and contributions from members of the group. You might just ask them to brainstorm what the word brings to mind, or have someone share a meditation on the word followed by an appropriate prayer. Since some of these locations close in the early afternoon, the walk is better made in the morning or between 3.00 p.m. and 5.00 p.m. in the later afternoon.

Directions are given after all the locations have been described.

1. *Last Supper in an Upper Room (the Cenacle)*

Luke 22:7–22 (Matthew 26:17–30; Mark 14:12–21; John 13:21–30)

The Cenacle is one of several places which have been believed to be the location of the Last Supper although it does not appear in tradition until the fifth century. The idea that this was the place is derived from the earlier tradition which places the Pentecost event in an upper room at that location. The conclusion was that it was the same upper room.

Music: 'Let Us Break Bread Together'
Word: FEAST

2. *Gethsemane and the arrest of Jesus (Garden of the Church of All Nations)*

Luke 22:39–53 (Matthew 26:17–30; Mark 14:32–50)

'Gethsemane' means 'oil press' and there is no doubt that this olive grove is the general area in which Jesus was betrayed, since the name has not changed over the centuries. The specific spot eludes Christians because wooded areas do change and there is great doubt that any of the olive trees could still be from the first century. The Romans cut down the trees in the whole area of the Mount of Olives to provide timber for the siege of AD 70. It is said, though, that every hole in the trunk of an olive tree represents ten years of growth and you might try counting the holes to come up with an age. There is also a cave nearby next to the Tomb of the Virgin Mary reputed to be where the disciples slept.

Music: 'Stay With Me' (words and music on page 130)
Word: PRAYER

3. The walk across the Kidron valley under arrest (called the Last Path)

Jesus was now under arrest and awaiting the judgement of the religious and state authorities. This valley holds the brook which divides Jerusalem on the west and the Mount of Olives on the east. As Jesus walked across the Kidron valley and looked around, he may well have remembered other scenes in his life such as:

- His time in the Temple at age 12. (Luke 2:40–52)
- The time when Satan brought him to the pinnacle (the south-east corner of the Temple compound) and tempted him to throw himself down to be rescued by angels. (Luke 4:9–13)
- The times when he taught people standing on the steps just outside the Huldah Gate (double gate visible in the south wall). (Luke 19:45–48)
- The numerous trips back and forth across the Kidron valley to visit his friends in Bethany.
- Or did the tombs remind him of his impending death? They were there when Jesus crossed the valley.

Music: As you walk, sing familiar hymns, stopping occasionally to think about what Jesus' memories might have been.
Word: JUDGEMENT

4. Peter's denial (Church of St Peter in Gallicantu)

Luke 22:31–34, 54–62 (Matthew 26:31–35, 69–75; Mark 14:27–31, 66–72; John 13:36–38; 18:15–18, 25–27)

The church of St Peter in Gallicantu (St Peter at the Crowing of the Cock) is modern but it encloses cellars, cisterns and stables from the Herodian period (37 BC–AD 70). For many centuries this was thought to be the house of Caiaphas. Since the scriptures placed Peter's denial in the same location as the house of Caiaphas, this might be that house (see page 72).

Music: 'Jesus, Remember Me' (words and music on page 130)
Word: REJECTION

5. Trial at the house of Caiaphas (benches facing unfinished Armenian Church on Mount Zion)

Luke 22:63–71 (Matthew 26:57–68; Mark 14:53–65; John 18:1–13)

The area known today as Mount Zion was the Upper City where the officials lived in Jesus' day. Although the present location of St Peter in Gallicantu was pointed out as the house of Caiaphas for many years, it was realized that it was more likely that Caiaphas resided in the upper-class neighbourhood now called Mount Zion. Evidence of wealthy homes from the first century was found in the Armenian cemetery on Mount Zion.

Music: 'Kyrie Eleison' (words and music on page 131)
Word: CONSPIRACY

6. The trial before Pilate (the Citadel)

Luke 23:1–25 (Matthew 27:11–31; Mark 15:1–20; John 18:28 – 19:16)

When Pontius Pilate came to Jerusalem, a backwater town, from the capital at Caesarea Maritima, he stayed in Herod's palace. The exact location is somewhat in doubt but the place now called the Citadel at Jaffa Gate seems to have the most in its favour. According to the custom of the day, there would have been a chair on a platform out in the open air with a plaza or paved area for onlookers.

Music: 'O Lord, Hear My Prayer' (words and music on page 131)
Word: AUTHORITY

7. On the way to Golgotha (old paving stones on Christian Quarter Road)

Luke 23:26–32 (Matthew 27:32–34; Mark 15:24–47; John 19:17)

Since the Romans often paraded prisoners through the city on the way to execution, the route taken might have meandered all over the city. Herod set the city up in a grid pattern and the present David Street is close to the path of one of the east–west streets ending at the Temple Mount in that day. Given the location of the walls at the time, Christian Quarter Road would have simply been a part of the territory outside the walls. The paving stones are from the end of the Roman period after the new walls were built, but the stones are of a style similar to those of the first century.

Music: 'Lest we forget Gethsemane' (words on page 132)
Word: LONELINESS

8. The crucifixion and burial (near the Church of the Holy Sepulchre)

Luke 23:33–57 (Matthew 27:35–61; Mark 15:24–47; John 19:16–30, 38–42)

There is very good evidence that the Church of the Holy Sepulchre is in the right place but over the centuries questions have been raised as to whether this location was really outside of the city walls. See page 44 above.

Music: 'Were You There When They Crucified My Lord?'
Word: DEATH

9. The Resurrection is reported to the disciples (either at St Mark's Syrian Orthodox Church or at the Cenacle)

Luke 24:1–12 (Matthew 28:1–10; Mark 16:1–8; John 20:1–18)

Along with the Cenacle, the Syrian Orthodox Church of St Mark also lays claim to be on the location of the Upper Room. Tradition suggests it as the house of Mary, the mother of St

Mark, as well as the location of Pentecost and the Last Supper. If so, it becomes a possible place for the disciples to have gathered after they fled the scene of the crucifixion. See page 8.

Music: 'Jesus Christ Is Risen Today' or another Easter favourite.
Word: DAWN

DIRECTIONS FOR THE HOLY WEEK WALK

1. The Cenacle is on Mount Zion. Go out Zion Gate and go straight ahead then right at the first fork in the path. Down the path there will be two signs high on the building saying 'coenaculum' to the left and Dormition Church to the right. Go left. The most prominent markings are for the Diaspora Yeshiva but there is a door marked ENTER in red. Go in and up the stairs following signs until you reach a large room. This is the traditional place of the Upper Room. You are not allowed to worship there; so go down and out towards Zion Gate where you will find some trees and stone benches.

2. Gethsemane and the grotto are at the foot of the Mount of Olives across the Kidron valley. If you are beginning with this location it is suggested that you go out St Stephen's Gate and down the hill. Turn right. The garden and the Church of All Nations are easy to recognize by sight.

3. Leaving the area to go toward the Church of St Peter in Gallicantu, stand with your back toward the steps of the Church of All Nations and turn left. Cross the street and take the path across the Kidron valley. It has recently been dubbed 'The Last Path'. This is a long journey. Stop several times to rest and to talk about what Jesus might have thought walking here under arrest.

4. 'The Last Path' returns to the roadway. After looking back to see where you have come, continue to the Church of St Peter in Gallicantu. Jesus would probably have walked directly to the spot and up the old stairway just below the present church. You may want to stand in one of the courtyards to remember Peter's denial or, with permission, in the chapel.

5. Go up the driveway from St Peter in Gallicantu and cross the street at the entrance to the Zion Gate car park. Walk through the car park up to the top and turn left. Take the same road you took to the Cenacle but you don't want to go very far at all. There are benches facing the unfinished Armenian church and the probable location of the house of Caiaphas.

6. Go through Zion Gate and enter the Old City. Turn left and follow Armenian Patriarchate Road, around the curve, past the Armenian convent to the Citadel (Tower of David Museum). There is an open plaza in front.

7. After the stop at the Citadel continue straight ahead through the plaza to David Street. It is a steep street through souvenir stores. Go down to Christian Quarter Road and turn left. About half way along the street you will see some large paving stones. They are from the end of the Roman Empire and have been raised up here in place. Stop there for the reading.

8. Continue to the next street and turn right. The Mosque of Omar is straight ahead but follow the turns in the road and go down the steps into the parvis (courtyard) of the Church of the Holy Sepulchre. You cannot hold prayers or sing songs there; so continue out through the archway on the other side into the open area by the Church of the Redeemer for worship.

9. If you are going to St Mark's Syrian Orthodox Church for the Upper Room where the disciples might have been waiting, go back up to Christian Quarter Road and turn left. When you reach David Street, cross it and go up the steps through a clothing shop onto St Mark's Road. Continue on St Mark's Road and when you see the door to the Lutheran Hospice, turn right. The road will lead you to St Mark's Syrian Orthodox Church. See page 8.

You might instead go back to the Upper Room at the Cenacle.

The easiest way is to retrace your steps, go back out Zion Gate and follow the directions above.

A Nativity journey

Although Bethlehem is the centre of the Nativity story, there are other locations within driving distance that are part of the biblical birth narrative. You will need transportation to undertake this whole journey. The section about Bethlehem following this one speaks of more current experiences you might also have in this town.

1. The ancestry of Jesus

Matthew 1:1–17 traces Jesus' ancestry beginning with Abraham, through Jacob, Ruth and Boaz, David and finally Joseph, 'the husband of Mary, of whom Jesus was born'. Luke's genealogy, coming at the point when Jesus was 30 (Luke 3:23–38), traces the lineage back from Joseph, through David, Boaz, Jacob and Abraham, to Adam, son of God. The Bethlehem area includes traces of these parts of Jesus' ancestry.

Just south of the Israeli military checkpoint on the Hebron Road is Rachel's Tomb, behind a high wall. Rachel, the wife of Jacob, died on the road to Bethlehem (Genesis 35:16–20) and the tomb has been a pilgrimage site for Jews, Christians and Muslims over the centuries. At present it is a Jewish synagogue and yeshiva.

Following Manger Street (left at the fork), a sign for David's Well is on the right. Look for a gate nearby with the year 1961 and a Jerusalem cross on one side and the Franciscan symbol on the other. Walk up the zigzag staircase and ask to see the sites. This is the only site in Bethlehem specifically connected to David (ancestor of Jesus) who was born and grew up in that city.

In one of David's battles with the Philistines, he was reported as saying 'O that someone would give me water to drink from the well of Bethlehem that is by the gate!' (2 Samuel 23:15). When given the water, David poured it out on the ground to honour God. Three cisterns mark the place where David's warriors broke through the Philistine lines and obtained water.

In addition to the three cisterns, there are catacombs of a Byzantine monastery, a Byzantine mosaic floor and recreational facilities owned by Catholic Action. Catholic Action is a social club and sports centre with basketball, volleyball and ping-pong on offer, as well as the only remaining cinema in Bethlehem. There are Christian catacombs under the building with about 80 tombs of monks who served the Byzantine monastery and church.

A phone call, in advance, to Catholic Action will reserve a meal for the group and will also assure that the gates are open and someone is there to show you around. They can also tell you about how this institution is helping today's people of Bethlehem.

If you go to the eastern side of the platform of David's Well, you can see the fields of Ruth and Boaz, as recounted in the Book of Ruth. Ruth, a Moabite, left her own people to accompany her mother-in-law, Naomi, to the Bethlehem area where she married Boaz. Obed, their son, was David's grandfather. This is also a good place to view, in advance, the Fields of the Shepherds in what is now called Beit Sahour (see pages 80–2).

Contact point *Catholic Action: tel. 02-274 3277*

2. The announcement of Jesus's birth

Although the annunciation took place in Nazareth, Mary first shared the good news with her cousin, Elizabeth, in the area called Ein Karem or Ain Karem (spring or fountain in the vineyards), north-west of Bethlehem. This is the traditional home of Elizabeth, her husband Zechariah, the priest, and their son, John the Baptist, where Mary visited Elizabeth (Luke 1:39–56). The words known as the Magnificat were spoken here. New roads are being built in this area; so check with local people for directions.

The Church of St John the Baptist boasts no famous paintings or statues but rather it is the location of fine paintings done by disciples of famous artists. If you walk through the sacristy into the exposition you will find a musty room with a partially labelled display of valuable and insignificant objects. One of the most unusual objects is a *communichino* – tongs used for the distribution of Holy Communion to 'people bearing pest disease'!

If you go out the door marked WC you will find another museum of household objects. Since the present church was completed in 1674, the collection is probably simply 300 years of throw-aways.

The Church of the Visitation, which is across the road and up the hill, has a very modern Upper Church with paintings of women in pastel colours. Some are singing and rejoicing and others represent specific women of the Bible or angelic virtues. The mosaic floor depicts birds, animals, grain and fruit as a tribute by nature to Mary. The lattice work on the windows is reminiscent of the lattice work used to hide women in traditional Eastern homes.

3. Mary's journey to Bethlehem

Return to Bethlehem from Ein Karem via the Hebron Road. There is an archaeological dig in the olive grove on the left side of the road, north of Mar Elias Monastery, designed to recover and develop the area known as the Kathisma of the Mother of God (or 'Bir Kadismu' which means 'well of resting'). This is where Mary is said to have rested on her way to give birth in Bethlehem.

The incident is mentioned in the Christian apocrypha. It relates that Mary, before she gave birth to Jesus, saw a vision while riding on a mule halfway between Jerusalem and Bethlehem. She saw a group of people rejoicing and another group mourning. After her husband Joseph asked her what was wrong, she told him, dismounted from the mule and rested on the rock. The rock was already a major pilgrimage site by the middle of the second century. In the fifth century a church was built around the rock, known in Greek as the *kathisma* or seat. Archaeologists believe it to be one of the biggest ever built in the Holy Land. Although it was destroyed around the beginning of the eleventh century, much of the elaborate mosaic floor is still intact. Excavations of the site began in the early 1990s. Today the Greek Orthodox Church, which owns the land, plans to develop the site into a major tourist attraction.

Another tradition about the place is that when the wise men approached Bethlehem after their stop in Jerusalem, they found it difficult to find the star again. One of them stopped for a drink from a well and the star was reflected on the surface of the water allowing them to continue on their way. Called 'Bir en-Nijm' or Well of the Star, it is located in the same place. By the middle of the second century, this was also a major pilgrimage stop.

Just after you pass Mar Elias Monastery on the left you will see a large building on the hill to your right just past the traffic light. It is called Tantur, Arabic for 'hilltop'. After Pope Paul VI's 1964 pilgrimage to the Holy Land, he purchased the Tantur terrain, then leased it to an ecumenical board. The Tantur Ecumenical Institute for Theological Studies was opened in 1971 as an international institute for theological research and pastoral studies and to encourage deeper understanding between Christians and peoples of different cultures. The Institute has a large library and organizes lectures and informal discussions which are open to the public.

Legend tells us that Mary had her first labour pains here, although if you look down into the valley on your left you will see a row of olive trees which was more likely to have been the road that Mary and Joseph took.

Contact point *Tantur Ecumenical Institute: tel. 02-676 0911, fax 02-676 0914*

4. The Fields of the Shepherds

After passing through the Israeli military checkpoint and passing Rachel's Tomb, bear left at the fork, follow the main road around the side of the hill. Turn left toward Beit Sahour ('the house of vigilance') just before the road up to Manger Square. People sometimes are cynical about the fact that three places are claimed as Shepherds' Fields. A reading of Luke 2:8–20, however, does not in any way preclude groups of shepherds all over the area and the multitude of the heavenly host could easily be heard by all. It was also not unusual for flocks of several owners to be gathered together with shepherds co-operating to keep track of the one larger flock, especially at night. Perhaps there are even more places that could be called Shepherds' Fields.

The Shepherds' Field is located in Beit Sahour. Its name reportedly stems from the Canaanite words *beit* meaning 'place' and *sahour* meaning 'night watch'. The name reflects the town's importance for shepherds as a grazing site during daytime and the safety the abundant caves offered to the flocks at night. Today Beit Sahour is a Christian town with a Muslim minority.

Fourth-century remains at both the Greek and Latin sites attest to early veneration of the area. The diary of Egeria, a pilgrim of the late fourth century, indicates a cave and altar and archaeologists have found remains of a site occupied by first-century nomadic shepherds. The murals inside the church at the Latin site were painted in the 1950s using people from Beit Sahour as models. You might even see a familiar face there, as many of the same families live in the area today.

The Greek Orthodox Church at the site of the Shepherds' Fields sits in a narrow, shallow valley that, according to tradition, is also known as the Fields of Boaz. Ruins of an earlier fourth-century church are located alongside the wonderfully painted modern Greek Orthodox Church, which was completed in 1989.

The East Jerusalem YMCA makes no claim to authenticity for its spot but it has built a Rehabilitation Centre to the side of their field. Pilgrims are welcome to each site and to visit the Rehabilitation Centre, which was set up for those wounded during the Intifada, the Palestinian uprising which began in December 1987 against the Israeli occupation. The centre consists of a counselling unit and a vocational training unit including carpentry, upholstery, tailoring, computers and secretarial work and art.

Contact point *YMCA Rehabilitation Centre: tel. 02-277 2713, fax 02-277 2203*

5. Manger Square and the Church of the Nativity

The present Church of the Nativity is one of the earliest Christian structures, originally erected in the fourth century by the Emperor Constantine. It was completely destroyed in the Samaritan revolt of 529 and was replaced during the reign of Justinian (527–565) on the same site.

Today, the compound of the Nativity church covers an area of approximately 12,000 square metres and includes, besides the Basilica, the Latin Convent in the north, the Greek Convent in the south-east and the Armenian Convent in the south-west.

The main entrance is by the very small Door of Humility. This entrance was made during the Ottoman era to prevent mounted horsemen from entering the Basilica.

The church is built over the site where Christ is traditionally said to have been born in a manger. Early writers refer to the cave, and not the stable, where Jesus was born. This is in keeping with the fact that both people and animals often lived in caves in the Bethlehem area at the time of Jesus. Indeed, there are people living in Bethlehem today who remember using a cave as the family house in their childhood, and a few are still living in caves in the town. It was also common to shelter animals in the basement of ancient Bethlehem homes. The Arab Women's Union has established a museum of such a house close to Manger Square.

The centre piece of the church is, of course, the Grotto of the Nativity, marking the site of Jesus' birth. An altar was erected over the birthplace and a fourteen-pointed silver star embedded in the white marble to mark the actual place. It is lit by fifteen silver lamps representing the different Christian communities. Six of the lamps belong to the Greek Orthodox, four to the Catholics and five to the Armenian Orthodox.

Three steps lead down to the altar of the manger where the baby Jesus was laid after he was born. Opposite the manger is an altar dedicated to the Wise Men, who came from the east to Bethlehem under the guidance of a star. It is on this altar that the Catholics celebrate their services, while the Greek and Armenian Orthodox celebrate theirs at the altar of the Nativity.

Notice the two icons of the Nativity in the Greek Orthodox area of the main church. One has in it a midwife getting ready to bathe the baby Jesus but first testing the water for the right temperature. In contrast to Western paintings, which often portray the birth of Jesus as a touching family scene, Eastern icons of the Nativity, like this one, are meant to show the faith and teaching of the Church about the Incarnation. Icons of biblical or Church history events can often seem complex or confusing as they include several scenes in one icon: time is not shown as linear but the whole event is portrayed at once to illustrate the significance and the theology of the event. Try to read it like a visually condensed sermon. Follow the pictures. The child, for example, is in the crib, placed outside a cave which is dark to foreshadow the tomb. Mary, the Mother of God, is resting. The shepherds feature as part of the central scene because their role is to witness and proclaim the tidings of great joy. Angels proclaim the message from the mountain and the Wise Men, still on horseback, are following the star.

Near the bottom of the icon are two additional scenes. Joseph is shown separated from the birth, plagued by doubts and concerned about his honour. In Eastern nativity icons there is also sometimes an old shepherd before Joseph, occasionally sprouting the small horns or the short tail of a devil. The other scene, which first appears in fifth-century icons, clearly identifies Jesus as human. Like any other baby, he must be bathed after he is born, and so the midwives take up the task.

The icon therefore visually teaches us the meaning of the Incarnation: Jesus, the son of God, takes on human form, born as a baby, to fulfil a divine mission on the Cross.

Adjacent to the Basilica is the Franciscan Church of St Catherine of Alexandria, which was built in 1881. This is where the Catholic midnight Christmas Mass is held and broadcast live by satellite to TV networks all over the world. It has a thriving Catholic congregation – join them on Sunday morning for worship (see below for contact number). There is also a daily procession of Franciscan fathers from St Catherine's to the Basilica at noon. The Basilica is open daily from 5.30 a.m. to 6.30 p.m.

One of the biggest disappointments of Christians of this land is that people come and view the holy sites without any acknow-ledgement of the Christians who have lived and worshipped there from the time of the first Apostles. A Palestinian friend once confided that he cannot read the Bible or Church history as something that happened somewhere else. He has lived in the Bible. The towns are his towns; he climbed the hills in his childhood and worshipped in the churches tourists come to photograph. Although a modern-day visitor cannot share that experience, Bethlehem is a place where Christians should consider joining local Christians at worship.

See the Christian Information Centre (page 125) for a list of Bethlehem churches and times of worship. Turn also to the chapter on Christian celebrations for special services and processions at the three Christmas seasons.

Contact point *Franciscan Church of St Catherine of Alexandria: tel. 02-274 2425*

6. The flight to Egypt

If you are going into the Sinai on the way to Cairo there are many locations commemorated as the Holy Family's stops along the way. One of the most popular is the Milk Grotto Church, five minutes' walk south-east of Manger Square, along Milk Grotto Street.

Tradition has it that the Holy Family made a hurried stop here during the flight to Egypt and, in the rush, a drop of Mary's milk fell to the ground while she was breastfeeding, turning the rock from red to white. Christians and Muslims alike have since believed that the rock increases a nursing mother's milk and a woman's fertility. In a country where a premium is put on having children, women of both faiths come here to pray.

1 The new dome of
   the Church of the
   Holy Sepulchre is
   an important
   symbol of unity

2 His Beatitude
   Michel Sabbah,
   Latin Patriarch of
   Jerusalem, in the
   courtyard of the
   Church of St
   Anne's in
   Jerusalem following
   the Palm Sunday
   procession

3 Patriarch Diodoros
   I, Greek Orthodox
   Patriarch of
   Jerusalem

4 Dome of the Greek
   Catholic (Melkite)
   Church in the
   Greek Catholic
   Patriarchate

5 The Romanian Orthodox Patriarchate
6 The Syrian Orthodox Scouts, on Christmas Eve in Bethlehem

7 *Ceremony of the Holy Fire at the Church of the Holy Sepulchre, Jerusalem*

8 *Greek Orthodox procession, during the Feast of the Dormition (Assumption) of the Virgin Mary*

9 The Washing of the Feet on Maundy Thursday at the parvis of the Holy Sepulchre, by His Beatitude Diodoros I, Greek Orthodox Patriarch of Jerusalem

10 Coptic priest at the Coptic Chapel behind the edicule in the Holy Sepulchre

11 Coptic crosses on the hood of a Coptic priest

12 Interior of St. George's Anglican Cathedral, Jerusalem

13 The Sunbula craft shop at St Andrew's Hospice, Jerusalem
14 Russian Orthodox nuns at the Tomb of the Virgin Mary at
    Gethsemane

15 Russian
Orthodox
priests on
Orthodox Palm
Sunday

16 Armenian
priest

17 *Armenians at St James's Cathedral on Easter Sunday*

18 Crowds
gathering on
Christmas Eve
in Bethlehem

19 Ethiopian girls'
choir at Easter

20 *Ethiopian monks on the rooftop of the Church of the Holy Sepulchre*
21 *A mural in the Chapel of the Angels at the Latin site of the*
    Shepherds' Fields in Beit Sahour

22 *Icon of the Virgin Mary breast-feeding the infant Jesus at the Milk Grotto in Bethlehem*

23 *A Muslim woman praying at the site of the Holy Manger in the Grotto of the Church of the Nativity, Bethlehem*

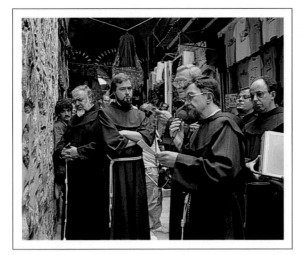

24 Franciscans at the Eighth Station of the Cross along the Via Dolorosa

25 The Eleventh and Twelfth Stations of the Cross, inside the Church of the Holy Sepulchre

26 *Easter Sunday Service at the Garden Tomb, Jerusalem*

27 *Greek Orthodox Easter Sunday Procession to the Church of the Holy Sepulchre*

28 *A Palestinian woman in traditional dress under an olive tree*

29 *An icon of the Virgin Mary and Jesus as a child*

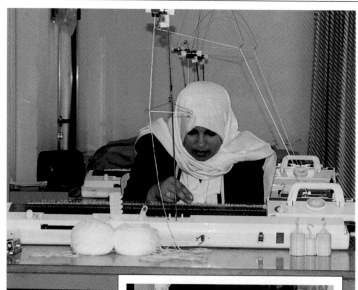

30 *Palestinian woman at the Near East Council of Churches' (NECC) self-help sewing programme in Gaza*

31 *Children outside the NECC health clinic in Darraj, Gaza*

The church's Franciscan priest has a supply of small vials of the crushed stone which some women take away to drink in powdered form.

Local Catholic women meet here every week to worship together. Why not join them? Check the time by calling the church (see below for number). The church is open daily from 8 a.m. to 11.45 a.m. and 2 p.m. to 6 p.m.

Contact point *Tel. 02-274 3867*

Bethlehem today and into the twenty-first century

B ethlehem is much more than the Church of the Nativity and the other holy sites. Founded probably 5,000 years ago, Bethlehem has existed for more years before the nativity of Jesus than after it. It was a major stop on pilgrim routes from the early years of the Christian era with convents, monasteries and private homes providing accommodation. Even today, it is first of all a hometown to Christians and Muslims, complete with markets, schools, restaurants and all the other infrastructure needed in a residential town. Accommodation today also includes good hotels and there are excellent restaurants. The 'little town' of Bethlehem, along with Beit Jala to the west and Beit Sahour to the east, make up the Bethlehem District, still referred to by some as the Christian triangle.

For most of the centuries since the nativity, the towns of the Bethlehem District were almost completely Christian. After 1947, Bethlehem itself became increasingly Muslim owing to the arrival of refugees and the establishment of refugee camps. Emigration to the West of both Christians and Muslims, particularly of the educated middle class, as well as the higher birth rate among Muslims, has meant that the town is now more than 60 per cent Muslim. Many of its original Christian inhabitants are to be found today in South America and other places. There are, for example, 300,000 immigrants from the Bethlehem area in Chile.

Bethlehemites are hospitable people, so alongside visiting the ancient stones, take time to meet the 'living stones'.

1. Visit and attend worship at the local churches

English is taught in the schools and many adults speak good English. If you attend a worship service, therefore, stay afterwards to meet the local people and partake in whatever hospitality is offered. See the Christian Information Centre for names of churches and times of worship services (page 125).

2. Meet with students

Bethlehem University is sponsored by the Vatican and was established after the visit of Pope Paul VI to the Holy Land in 1964. Opened in 1973, it provides education and vocational training for over 2,000 Christians and Muslims, with courses ranging from hotel management to midwifery. Conversations with students or staff can be arranged.

Bethlehem Bible College is a Christian training centre for Arabic-speaking youth aspiring to be pastors, Christian educators, counsellors and youth directors. It also runs a tour guide programme that helps train and provide licensed and qualified guides in anticipation of an increasing number of tourists. Visitors to the school are welcome.

The College also runs a small shop selling olive wood products at reasonable prices. Call in advance to check it will be open. They will also provide lunch for groups on request.

Contact points
Bethlehem University: tel. 02-274 1241/1242/1243, fax 02-274 4440
Bethlehem Bible College: tel. 02-274 1190, fax 02-274 3278

3. Visit an institution

The International Centre of Bethlehem is located in the Lutheran Evangelical Christmas Church. The Centre was founded by Rev. Dr Mitri Raheb, the pastor and author of the book *I Am a Palestinian Christian* (Minneapolis: Fortress Press,

1995). Along with travel planning and accommodation, it sponsors a women's studies programme, lectures, cultural programmes, youth programmes and a reintegration programme for young Palestinian graduates of foreign universities as well as German–Palestinian student exchanges. In early 1998 the corner stone was laid for Dar al-Kalima, a Palestinian theological Academy. The Academy will include a Centre for Music and Art in downtown Bethlehem and a School for Intercultural Studies on nearby Murier Mountain. All are welcome to visit the Centre and hear more about its plans and its work.

The International Centre of Bethlehem also runs the Abu (Jubran) Guest House which is a good way to enjoy local hospitality and culture.

Contact point *Tel. 02-277 0047, fax 02-277 0048,*
e-mail: annadwa@planet.edu   website http://www.planet.edu/
annadwa/homepage.htm

Wi'am Palestinian Conflict Resolution Centre, directed by an articulate and committed Christian named Zoughbi Zoughbi, helps mediate conflicts and sponsors workshops on such topics as bringing up children, the challenges of early marriage, and male–female relations in a predominantly male society. The staff is kept very busy owing to the stress local people experience because of political problems including the difficulty in getting permits from the Israeli army to enter Jerusalem to work or visit holy sites for worship. Bethlehem is often subject to Israeli military closure, restricting freedom of movement for many of its population. If they have time, members of the centre's staff are willing to meet with groups.

Contact point *Tel./fax 02-277 0513*

Al Liqa' (Encounter) Centre for Religious and Heritage Studies in the Holy Land is dedicated to the study of Christian–Muslim relations, interfaith dialogue in the Palestinian context and to other local issues. Visitors are welcome.

Contact point *Tel./fax 02-274 1639*

The Centre for Rapprochement Between Peoples in Beit Sahour was started in 1988 during the Intifada under the auspices of the Mennonite Central Committee in Jerusalem to bring about dialogue between Israeli Jews and Palestinians (Christians and Muslims). Beit Sahour was internationally known as the town that engaged in tax resistance and non-violent civil disobedience. That led to strict Israeli curfews and the confiscation of household possessions along with business goods.

Contact point *Tel./fax 02-277 2018*

Many schools, homes for children and other social service agencies in the area are sponsored by churches or international church-related groups. Many such agencies are very happy to have groups come but visits should be arranged in advance. Some possibilities are: Hope Secondary School and Talitha Kumi School in Beit Jala; Bishop Gabriel School in Beit Sahour; Terra Sancta School and Frères School in Bethlehem. There is also a Caritas Hospital for Children and an SOS Children's Village in Bethlehem. More complete lists of Christian schools and Christian-sponsored social services are available through the Christian Information Centre (see page 125).

4. View the making of products

Bethlehem is famous for its souvenirs from olive wood. It is believed that the craft was begun in Bethlehem in the fourth century following the construction of the Church of the Nativity at which time the monks taught the craft to the local residents. Franciscan friars from Damascus are credited with establishing the mother-of-pearl industry in Bethlehem between the fourteenth and sixteenth centuries. To teach local residents, they brought in craftsmen from Genoa. The Bethlehem area today includes 63 olive wood and 56 mother-of-pearl workshops or factories.

Factories where olive wood carvings are produced piece by piece are located in several places in town, especially along Milk

Grotto Street. Workers are usually willing to tell you about their craft, talk about the olive wood and demonstrate their tools.

Jesus said 'I am the bread of life'. One translation of Bethlehem is 'house of bread' and bakeries with venerable ovens abound, especially in the older part of town. The best time to visit is early in the morning to watch and then purchase fresh *pita* or *kaik*, an oval-shaped loaf covered with sesame seeds and often eaten while walking about the streets.

5. Explore museums of folklore

For those interested in costume, household articles and folklore, there are currently two museums with plans for more by the year 2000. The Palestinians who own and operate these museums are very happy to talk with you about life in this area, past and present.

Maha Saca, the owner of the Palestinian Heritage Centre (near the Paradise Hotel in Bethlehem), has been collecting Palestinian clothing and artefacts for many years. At the museum you will see men's garb and the beautifully embroidered black or white dresses that women traditionally wore and treasured. Each village had its own patterns and colours of decoration and headdress. Married Bethlehem women wore a high hat called a *shatweh*, decorated with gold coins and covered with a white cloth, and elaborately embroidered dresses.

The Old Bethlehem Home (on an alley about 50 metres west of Manger Square) houses traditional Bethlehem clothing, furniture and household items displayed by the Arab Women's Union of Bethlehem. Here you can see a traditional living room, bedroom and kitchen in one of the oldest types of architecture in Bethlehem as well as exhibition rooms containing costumes and jewellery. A new museum is under construction on the Hebron Road.

6. Visit a living monastery

On a scale drawn between living stones and ancient stones, monasteries are very much at the ancient end. The Holy Land is full of the ruins of these venerable institutions. But modern convents and monasteries exist, filled with monks and nuns from international orders. There are also ancient monasteries which are still living and welcome visitors (sometimes only men) with traditional hospitality.

The Judean desert was one of the most important centres of monasticism in the fourth and fifth centuries, with hundreds of dwellings and thousands of monks. The desert held many natural springs and caves providing both solitude and a hiding place from persecution. In many desert monasteries (called *laura*), monks lived a solitary life during the week and met together for communal prayer and Mass at weekends. But monasteries based on a communal life (called *coenobium*) were also established and became destinations for pilgrims and places of hospitality for travellers. There were monasteries in or near cities, as well as mountainous areas but the desert monasteries were the best known. Most monasteries were wiped out in the seventh century as a result of the Persian invasion. There was however a revival in the nineteenth century and a few old monasteries still exist and can be visited. In the Judean desert east of Bethlehem there is Mar Saba and St Theodosius. On the road to Jericho there is St George in Wadi Kelt and the Monastery of the Holy Cross in Jerusalem is just down the hill from the Knesset, the Israeli Parliament.

7. Plans for the celebration of AD 2000

Since the year 2000 celebrates the bi-millenary of the nativity of Jesus Christ, the town of Bethlehem is a major focal point for that celebration. Plans are already under way to restore and renovate the city ready for the millennium and the expected influx of tourists. Roads, water pipes, buildings and other forms of infrastructure were sadly neglected in the 30 years of Israeli military occupation, so there is much catching up to be done.

Repairs and new buildings are also slowed down by the fact that Bethlehem is sometimes subject to military closure and construction materials cannot reach the area. Someone quipped that 'We will be ready by 2010!' Many local people, however, are looking at the millennium as the kick-off for a revival of the town. Under the motto 'Bethlehem – a town to rehabilitate together', restoration, rather than replacement, is being carried out in the older areas. Restoration has already begun on ancient arches and alleyways.

UNESCO (United Nations Educational, Scientific and Cultural Organization) has been involved in the planning stage for rehabilitation and an organ of the Palestine National Authority, called the 'Bethlehem 2000 Project', is co-ordinating the progress. The United Nations Development Programme is working with several countries on carrying out their projects. New projects are continuously emerging from local groups and both international involvement and private enterprises are being encouraged. In addition to infrastructure, the 'Bethlehem 2000 Project' is also working on plans for tourism as well as religious events during the Jubilee year. In some of this, close co-ordination is being maintained with local churches and the Middle East Council of Churches.

Some of the projects which have been planned for the 'Bethlehem 2000 Project' are:

- The transformation of Manger Square from an asphalt paved carpark into a tiled piazza with trees and fountains with help from Sweden.
- The replacement of the present cement block police station with a civic centre with an auditorium and a museum of art and religion, aided by Japan.
- A new central bus station.
- A new hotel and commercial complex incorporating an Arab mansion on Hebron Road near Rachel's Tomb.
- The rebuilding of the Municipal Market Place.
- The renovation of the Madbasa area on the west part of Paul VI Street with money from Germany.

The Christians of Bethlehem are looking forward to welcoming the anticipated five million tourists and pilgrims expected to visit the city for the year 2000. This is, after all, the focal point for the millennium celebrations as the site of Christ's birth.

One of the best guide books to Bethlehem is *Bethlehem 2000*, written by Sawsan and Qustandi Shomali, both lecturers at Bethlehem University. It is published by Flamm Druck Wagener GmbH. Visit the book's website on http://www.geocities.com/capitolhill/lobby/8856

Contact point *'Bethlehem 2000 Project': tel. 02-274 2224/5/6, fax 02-274 2227*

Nazareth

Nazareth is the town of the annunciation where the Angel Gabriel told the Virgin Mary that she would give birth to the Christ-Child. Nazareth was also the hometown of Jesus and it was here that he grew up and spent his early years. A pilgrimage to the Holy Land would therefore hardly be complete without a visit to this city and an encounter with today's Nazarenes.

That said, for many years, Nazareth has been considered too crowded and congested to warrant a stop and has often been overlooked by both tourists and tour guides alike. Today, however, Nazareth, like Bethlehem, is planning its own festivities for the year 2000 and preparing for what is hoped will bring an influx of tourists. A replica of biblical Nazareth is currently under construction on the grounds of the hospital run by the Scottish Edinburgh Medical Missionary Society. 'Nazareth Village' will include a full-scale reproduction of a first-century village and a living museum, which will present the life and teachings of Jesus. The project planners hope to have a good part of the village in place by the year 2000.

Already in preparation for the millennium, streets and roads are being widened, the old market area has been completely restored and a pedestrianized street, complete with street-lights, has recently been built between the Greek Orthodox Church of St Gabriel and the Latin-rite Roman Catholic Basilica of the Annunciation. The Basilica is the jewel and centrepiece of this largest Arab Christian city in Israel proper. Greek Orthodox form the largest Christian community, but there are also significant numbers of Latin Catholics, Greek Catholics and Maronites, plus an active Anglican Church.

The Church of the Annunciation stands over the ruins of

earlier Byzantine and Crusader structures; along with today's modern-day edifice, all were built over what tradition holds was the house of the Virgin Mary. The modern basilica was completed in 1969 and was funded by Roman Catholic communities the world over. Of particular interest are the wide range of mosaics found along the walls of the cloister, just before entering the church. All are gifts from Roman Catholic communities from around the world.

St Joseph's Church, also known as 'The Church of the Carpenter's Shop', is just next door to the Church of the Annunciation. Owned by the Franciscans, this church is also built over earlier Byzantine and Crusader ruins and is the reputed site of Joseph's carpentry shop and thus the home of the Holy Family. The current structure was built in 1914.

The Church of St Gabriel is built over the site of 'Mary's Well' where, according to tradition, the angel Gabriel first appeared to Mary. A nearby spring provides the water source for the 'Fountain of Mary'. Notice the blue Armenian tiles that decorate the lower parts of the church on approaching the well. These tiles were brought from Armenia by the Crusaders. The Greek Orthodox Church that now stands on this site was built in 1769 and was constructed over the earlier Crusader structure.

The Church of the Mensa Christi, one of Nazareth's little-known secrets, has only recently come back to life after many years of neglect. Built around a great rock known as Mensa Christi, or 'Table of the Lord', this church is said to be one of the sites where Jesus and his disciples dined following the Resurrection. This church was constructed by the Franciscans in 1861, and was recently restored by a team of twelve Italian women from the Venice School of Restoration.

A small and unassuming building of Crusader construction in the old marketplace of Nazareth and now owned by the Greek Catholic Church is said to be built over the site of the **Synagogue** where Jesus learned as a boy, and later where he taught and read the Scriptures.

Christ Church on Casa Nova Street is the Anglican Church in Nazareth, just steps away from the Church of the Annunciation.

This church incorporates both Arabic and English into the liturgy, and Holy Communion is celebrated on the first Sunday of each month. Services are held every Sunday morning beginning at 10.30 a.m. Call the church ahead of time if you have a group that would like to attend services. There is also an opportunity to meet and get to know local Christians over a cup of coffee and some Arabic sweets after the service.

Contact point *Tel. 06-655 4017, fax 06-656 3649*

Though Nazareth has many hotels and new ones are currently being constructed in Nazareth Illit, 'Upper Nazareth', why not stay in one of the many Christian-run hospices? They offer not only comfortable, clean, affordable accommodation, but many have spectacular panoramic views over the city. A few worthy of mention are:

Casa Nova – just beside the Church of the Annunciation, the dining room of this Franciscan hospice features authentic Italian cuisine. Tel. 06-645 6660, fax 06-657 9630.

St Gabriel Hotel – on the highest hill above Nazareth, this monastery-turned-hostel offers the best views of Nazareth and the surrounding countryside from the bell tower of its chapel. Tel. 06-656 7349, fax 06-655 4071.

St Margaret's Hostel – just below St Gabriel's, this Anglican-run hospice also offers great views of the city. The market of Old Nazareth is also within walking distance from here, straight down the hill. Tel. 06-657 3507, fax 06-656 7166.

During the last few centuries, Nazareth was surrounded by a large number of Christian villages, but few remain today. See **Ibillin** and **Shefar'am** in the chapter on Christian towns and villages. Also close by is the town of **Cana** which has a sizeable Palestinian Christian population today. This is where Jesus performed his first publicly recorded miracle – turning water into wine at a wedding feast. Visit the 'wedding church' at Cana today. Here many couples on pilgrimage renew their marriage vows. Marriage Encounter pennants from many different countries, autographed by thousands of couples, line the walls. Take some time to reflect on the central relationships in your life.

Sea of Galilee

In visiting Jerusalem, Bethlehem, Nazareth or Christian towns and villages, there's always the opportunity to encounter the 'living stones' of this land. In the Sea of Galilee area, there are few Christians except for Franciscan and Benedictine nuns and monks, mostly from other countries. Instead, this is an area of fun and sun for the Israelis and is especially crowded on Jewish holidays and on Shabbat (Saturdays).

Also unlike the cities above, there is no single focus for sites: not the birth of Jesus in Bethlehem; the trial, death and resurrection of Jesus in Jerusalem; nor the annunciation and early years of Jesus in Nazareth. Still this is the location of the principal part of Jesus' public life even though in most cases there is no specific proven site that has been historically attributed to teachings or healings. There is also no planned rationale for the places commemorated around the lake which make those events or teachings more important than others. Capernaum is accurate as a base for Jesus' work in the Galilee, but who really knows where on the lake Jesus walked? Many healings were on the way between places. But we do know that Jesus walked and sailed, taught and healed in this region. He experienced the land, wind, rain, seasons, soil, trees, flowers, rocks, and hills which make up the 'Fifth Gospel' and which can teach us along with the four Gospels of the Bible.

The details of the sites that are commemorated, mostly by twentieth-century churches, are available in any guidebook. The material below is designed to make the ancient stones and the land come alive for you. It is offered in a format of: (a) scripture and focus; (b) questions for your own thoughts or group discussion; (c) prayer suggestions.

1. Ginosar – first-century fishing boat

(a) (Luke 5:1–11): fishing on the lake

(b) Many other forms of fishing are used on the lake but fishing from a boat is a particularly dangerous occupation because of the weather, because it is often done at night and because of the possibility of capsizing. What are today's dangerous occupations? Where is the danger in what you do?

(c) Pray for those who risk themselves in their occupations, especially for the betterment of others.

2. Tabgha, Church of the Multiplication

(a) (John 6:1–13): using resources

(b) The learning for the disciples was not just that the people were fed but that they themselves could participate imaginatively in this miracle. When has your presence been a part of an important happening? What did you do to make it happen?

(c) Pray for those who use the earth's resources imaginatively and with care.

3. Tabgha, Church of Mensa Christi

(a) (John 21:1–17): 'Simon, do you love me?'

(b) Although Peter was called as a discile in the early days of Jesus' ministry, this was the time when Jesus called him to move from followership to leadership. What leadership role or followership role do you take in the life of the church?

(c) Pray for those who are called to serve Jesus Christ as leaders and as followers.

4. Mount of Beatitudes

(a) (Matthew 5:1–12): blessings for those without

(b) Jesus lived in a society where there was a line drawn between those who could keep the multitude of commandments and the common people whose occupation or lack of money kept them always 'unclean'. They were outside the society, but the blessings are unexpectedly directed to them. Who are those in your society who would be surprised by unexpected blessings?

(c) Pray for those who are outsiders in your society and the blessings they need.

5. Capernaum

(a) (Mark 1:29–31 and Mark 3:31–35): family, home

(b) After leaving his hometown of Nazareth, Jesus chose disciples and made the home of Peter his own home. Jesus had two families – the one of his birth and the family of disciples and followers. What groups or individuals outside of your blood relatives would you call 'family'? Why?

(c) Pray for the family of people you have chosen to be part of your life and for the special gifts they bring to you.

6. Kursi, restored ruins of Byzantine monastery

(a) (Mark 5:1–20): healing

(b) Jesus often healed people along the way, especially those who were not part of the righteous of the land (women, demoniacs, Roman soldiers, lepers). He disturbed the social order of his day by these healings. Who do you know who disturbs the social order today by their good deeds?

(c) Pray for those who have the courage to go beyond the rules and strictures to care for those considered unacceptable.

7. Yardenit, baptism site

(a) (Mark 1:4–11): renewal

(b) It is believed that Jesus was baptized in the Jordan river near Jericho but the area has been a closed military zone since 1967. Yardenit was set up in the Galilee as an 'alternative' baptism site and is a commercial enterprise run by a kibbutz. Think about the political realities that impact your visit to this area today.

(c) Pray for all the pilgrims seeking to know Jesus by visiting the Holy Land.

8. Cities around the lake

(a) (Matthew 5:14–16): light
(b) It is often said that there is a bias towards the countryside in Christian preaching and symbolism, yet Jesus spent much of his time in cities and towns – Jerusalem, Capernaum, the cities of the Decapolis and it is believed that he and Joseph worked in Sephoris, which was being built at that time. What does the idea of light coming from cities mean to you?
(c) Pray for city dwellers and the ways their light shines to the world.

9. The farmers of the Galilee, farming on the side of a hill

(a) (Luke 8:4–8): parable of the sower
(b) There are some very fruitful plains in the Galilee, so much so that it has been called the 'breadbasket' of Palestinian life. But farmers have also learned to grow crops on rocky hillsides by using terraces as in the parable. What are the greatest hazards for farmers in this area today?
(c) Pray for those who feed us by their working knowledge of agriculture.

10. Lake and water

(a) (Mark 4:35–41): stilling the storm
(b) The lake called Sea of Galilee or Sea of Tiberias or Lake Kinereth was the backdrop of many of Jesus' healings, teachings and miracles and we often picture it as quiet and idyllic. But a cold east wind called the Sharkiyeh can blow up quickly and endanger the lives of those on the lake. Where are there places today where the forces of nature have caused danger?
(c) Pray for those who have suffered from recent natural disasters and pray for the rebuilding of their lives.

Christian towns and villages off the tourist track

One way to get to know the Christians of the Holy Land is to visit towns and villages beyond the popular tourist sites. Over the centuries there were times when Christians were in the majority in the Holy Land and even in the early twentieth century there were a significant number of places that were entirely or mainly Christian. Many Christian villages were depopulated as a result of the 1948 war when their residents became refugees and the villages have since disappeared off the maps. Others still exist but have disappeared from the minds of visiting Christians. Below are listed a few of the locations where there is an English-speaking official or priest to help you. Sometimes more than one spelling appears in English since the name of a location is a transliteration of Arabic.

The number of Christians listed below was supplied by the Christian Information Centre from 1995 statistics. L means Latin Catholic; M means Melkite (Greek Catholic); G means Greek Orthodox; P means Protestant or Anglican.

Ramallah/El Bireh

Just north of Jerusalem, Ramallah and El Bireh are twin cities with many Christian families. El Bireh is older and was known as a major stopping point on the road from Jerusalem to the Galilee in the first century. This is probably the place where Jesus' family stopped and discovered him missing when he was twelve. Ramallah was one of the first places in the Holy Land where major schools were established by Christian churches, so it is a good place to visit schools and meet young people (Quaker schools are English-speaking).

Ramallah also houses the Educational Network, a non-governmental organization which provides information on Palestinian education and creates a channel for the improvement of the Palestinian education system.

The city is also a major business centre today with good hotels and well-known restaurants. A folklore museum at the Ina'ash El Usra in El Bireh contains a fine collection of bedouin and village clothing. Call the Quaker Upper School (also called Friends Boys' School) to visit or see the Christian Information Centre for other schools. Call the Lutheran Church of Hope to visit church groups.

There are 4,910 Christians of a variety of denominations with about 500 Protestants.

Contact points
Educational Network, Ramallah: tel. 02-295 6230
Quaker Upper School, El Bireh: tel. 02-295 6230
Lutheran Church of Hope, El Bireh: tel. 02-295 3447

Taybeh (Taibe)

Taybeh, near Ramallah, is one of only two completely Christian villages in the West Bank. The site has been occupied as a holy place since the Canaanite period and is traditionally the place where Jesus fled to avoid the authorities after the raising of Lazarus (John 11:54). A mosaic inside the Latin Catholic Church describes Jesus' entrance into the town. Taybeh is also the home of a micro brewery producing Taybeh beer (but not the town of Taybeh football fame). You can visit the brewery and also see Byzantine and Crusader church ruins. You can also go inside an old traditional house preserved as a museum as well as meet Christians who can trace their families back for centuries in this area. A hostel has been recently renovated and Mark Alphonso, manager of the Charles de Foucauld Centre (see below), can arrange for stays of up to 50 people. Call the Latin pastor, Fr

Butros Sleiman (see below), if you want to visit but not stay over.
L, M, G = 1,100.

Contact points
Charles de Foucauld Centre: tel. 02-295 2364
Fr Butros Sleiman: tel. 02-295 8020

Bir Zeit

Stay in Ramallah or Jerusalem to visit Bir Zeit where the main
interest is the University. Bir Zeit University was begun by the
Nasser family (a Palestinian Christian family) in the 1920s and
attained university status in the 1970s. It has a worldwide reputation
due to its academic excellence, its programmes for international
students and the persistent closures and arrests during the Intifada.
Call Albert Aghazarian of the University's Public Relations office to
visit the University of Bir Zeit or to meet with groups of students.
There is also a good Women's Studies Programme and lectures can
be arranged by calling in advance (see below). Bir Zeit University
has adopted an on-line travel guide 'The Ramallah Online Travel
Guide' (http://www.birzeit.edu/ramallah) as part of its own
website. The travel guide was researched and written by Bir Zeit
Palestine and Arabic Studies students and offers up-to-date travel
information on what to do in the region around the university, as
well as information on some of the Christian villages mentioned.
The guide includes information about museums, art galleries and
cultural centres, hotels, shops and restaurants.

Father Emile Salayta is the General Director of the Latin
Schools in the West Bank. He is also the Latin priest at Bir Zeit
Latin Convent. Contact the Latin Convent in Bir Zeit to arrange
an appointment with Fr Salayta and/or to visit the Latin church.
L, M, G, P = 1,560.

Contact points
Bir Zeit University: tel. 02-298 2258, 298 2059
Women's Studies Programme: tel. 02-298 2959
Latin Convent: tel./fax 02-295 7834

Jifna (Gifna)

Jifna is best visited as a day trip from Jerusalem since there are no hotel facilities. Along with Taybeh, Jifna is one of the only two remaining all-Christian villages in the West Bank. The name Jifna comes from *Gufna* in Aramaic and means 'vineyard'. Tradition has it that Judas Iscariot resided there. According to popular culture, it is thought that Mary and Joseph rested under the fig trees in Jifna on their way from Nazareth to Bethlehem. This tradition could well be authentic as the Roman road from north to south at the time passed through this village. L, G = 530.

Contact point *Fr Rafic Khoury: tel. 02-295 7873*

Aboud ('Abud)

On a day trip from Jerusalem you can visit 'Abud. The 1,000-strong Christian population is served by three churches – Greek Orthodox, Roman Catholic and Church of God. The village is famous for the feast of St Barbara on 17 December, when a special dish is served called *burbura* made from boiled, hulled wheat. The Greek Orthodox priest speaks English and the church is active.

Contact point *Fr Abdallah Sumrein, Church of St Mary (Aboud has no telephones)*

Hebron

Although not a Christian town, Hebron is home to the Christian Peacemaker Team, made up mostly of Church of the Brethren, Mennonite and Quaker Christians. They form a non-violent Christian presence working for peace and justice in this troubled town. Stay in Jerusalem and call ahead of time for directions and an appointment. The only other Christians in town are a small handful of Russian Orthodox nuns/monks at the Oak of Mamre.

Contact point *CPT: tel. 050-397 506 (mobile phone)*

Ramle

From the eighth century until Crusader times, Ramle was the principal Arab city of Palestine. In later times it accommodated pilgrims in a hospice on their trek from Jaffa to Jerusalem and was known as the home of Joseph of Arimathea. It is west of Jerusalem on Route 1. Here you can visit a renovated home called Open House, founded by Dahlia and Yehezkel Landau along with the Al-Khayri family. It was originally the Arab home of the Al-Khayri family before the 1948 war. It was then occupied by Dahlia Landau's family, a Jewish family from Bulgaria, as 'abandoned property'. Years later the two families met and decided to open the house as a sign of reconciliation and goodwill between Israelis and Palestinians. Today the House serves the local community with a day care centre, an Arab–Jewish Parents' Network and a Peace Camp for Jewish, Christian and Muslim youth. Here Jews and Arabs come to make friends, share activities and work together for peace.

The Executive Director is a Palestinian Christian with centuries-old roots in Ramle. L, M, G + other Catholic and Orthodox = 2678.

Contact point *Open House: tel. 08-922 1874, 02-642 3952*

Zababde

Zababde is about 40 minutes from Nazareth by car; there is no public transport. This is one of the few villages left in Israel with a Christian majority and the town can provide an opportunity for church services, folklore, *dabka* dancing (traditional Palestinian dancing), a home-cooked Arab dinner and meeting local people. There are also excavations in several towns nearby such as Bourquin, which is connected with the ten lepers, and Dothan, connected with the sale of Joseph. Contact Fr Louis Hazboun of the Latin church, who is also an archaeologist, to make arrangements. L, M, G, P = 1,630.

Contact point *Tel. 050-392 371 (mobile phone)*

Ibillin

This is the town and the school mentioned in the book *Blood Brothers* by Fr Elias Chacour, a Melkite priest who was driven out of Biram and spent years as a refugee. Biram, formerly a Christian village, does not exist any more as it was destroyed after the 1948 war. Ibillin is half Christian/half Muslim and the Mar Elias High School and College, which Fr Chacour built, are open to people of all religions. Students and teachers come from diverse backgrounds – Christian, Muslim, Druze and Jews – united in a dream of establishing a future pluralistic society.

There is currently a student exchange programme with several universities in Europe and the US as well as many international volunteers who come to the college, often sent by their church organizations.

There is also a unique monument at the school built as two semicircles with two stone benches inside. One says in Hebrew 'This is a memorial for the Palestinian Martyrs'; the other is in Arabic and says 'This is a memorial for the Jewish Martyrs'.

There is no overnight accommodation, though you can easily stay in Nazareth or Tiberias and enjoy the good restaurants of Ibillin. Make an appointment to see the school, although Fr Chacour travels and lectures around the world, so he may not be there when you are. You can also visit the two churches. M, G = 3,760.

Contact point *School office: tel./fax 04-986 6848; tel. 04-986 9490*

Shefar'am

Shefar'am, near Ibillin, is the location of the House of Hope, an international Christian peace centre focusing on Arab (Christian and Muslim)/Jewish relationships. House of Hope was founded by Elias Jabbour and offers visits to the centre as well as room-and-board facilities. House of Hope is also available for conferences. L, M, G, P = 6,800.

Contact point *Tel. 04-986 8558, fax 04-986 1211*

Gaza

Gaza is one of the oldest cities in the world. Archaeological evidence suggests that the Canaanites established communities in the Gaza area around 3000 BC. A reference in the first book of the Bible places Gaza firmly in Canaan (Genesis 10:19).

By the second millennium BC, Gaza was well established and was dominated in turn by the Babylonian and Assyrian empires. Around 1200 BC, it was settled by the Philistines who gave their name to the land – Philistia, a name which survives today in the word Palestine.

There are frequent references to Gaza and to the battles between the Philistines and the Israelites in the stories of the Old Testament. One of the most dramatic tales set in Gaza is the story of Samson, who is portrayed as a superhuman figure from the Israelite tribe of Dan, who was born to deliver the Israelites from misfortune (Judges 13).

In Judges 16, there is a foiled plot to ambush Samson as he leaves Gaza after a visit to a prostitute there. Here also is the well-known story of Samson and Delilah, the hair-cutting Philistine woman. Samson, shorn of his legendary strength, is seized by the Philistines, has his eyes gouged out and is bound in shackles in Gaza before he wreaks his revenge by causing a temple to fall on 3,000 Philistines.

Gaza was a flourishing centre of paganism up to and beyond the third century AD when Christianity took hold in the region. It is said that Christianity was first introduced to Gaza by the Apostle Philip, with Philemon serving as its first bishop.

It was through Gaza that the spirit of monasticism, which had grown and flourished in Egypt, was introduced to Palestine. The beginning of the fourth century was marked by the activities of

Hilarion, a leading figure in the history of Christianity in Gaza. He was born a few miles south of Gaza and studied in Alexandria. He returned to Palestine and led an ascetic's life of simplicity and prayer in the desert, establishing the first monastery in Palestine.

Christianity was formally adopted in Gaza at the end of the fourth century. Central to that was Porphyrios, who was appointed Bishop in 394. He waged a campaign against paganism in Gaza, eventually turning for help to the Roman Emperor Arcadius, who authorized the destruction of all pagan temples.

A large church, called the Eudoxiana, after the Emperor's wife, was built on the site of the popular local pagan god, Marnas. It survived until the seventh century when Islam arrived in Gaza and the church was converted into a mosque and renamed the Omari Mosque, or the Mosque of Omar.

Although most of Gaza's Christians became Muslim in the seventh century, some clung to their Christian faith, worshipping at the church where St Porphyrios was buried. Gaza's Greek Orthodox community continues to worship at this church, which was built in the middle of the fifth century.

Christian rule came briefly to Gaza in the middle of the twelfth century when Crusader forces captured the city. King Baldwin III handed responsibility for the city to the Knights Templar, who levelled the Omari Mosque, erecting in its place a church dedicated to St John the Baptist. When the Crusaders' short stay in Gaza ended, the church became a mosque once again. The present Omari Mosque retains several features of the building's Christian past: marble columns from the original Eudoxiana church, gothic arches, a cruciform font and a bell tower.

Gaza's Christians were all Greek Orthodox until the middle of the nineteenth century and the arrival of Roman Catholic missionaries. Today, there are around 200 Catholics and a church-run school for over 1,000 students. There are approximately 3,000 Christians in Gaza.

Christian pilgrims have been coming to Gaza since the fourth century. Why should you visit today? One reason is to share hospitality with local Gazan Christians who often feel forgotten by Christians from the West who focus their whole attention on the well-known holy sites of Jerusalem or the Galilee. Little is heard about the Christian community in Gaza, which has been true to its faith under severe political and economic pressures, recently experiencing a level of violence and hardship most of us find impossible to imagine. Many social programmes in Gaza are financed by churches and Christian organizations from around the world. Church-sponsored personnel and local Christians are at work throughout Gaza in its refugee camps, its hospitals and its training centres. An insight into their work is always a valuable experience, bringing you into contact with the realities of life in Gaza today as well as introducing you to the local Christian community. In addition, most pilgrims will say that it is often only after a visit to Gaza that they begin to appreciate the reality of the current Israeli–Palestinian conflict.

With the establishment of the State of Israel in 1948, three-quarters of the then Arab population of Palestine fled their homes. 200,000 found themselves refugees in the Gaza Strip, making the Strip today one of the most densely populated areas in the world: over one million people are crammed into 365 square kilometres, of which about 40 per cent is occupied by Jewish settlers.

Over 65 per cent of Gaza's population are refugees. About 55 per cent of those refugees live in the Strip's eight refugee camps. Unemployment is over 65 per cent, and 60 per cent of the population is under twenty.

During 27 years of occupation, Gaza was renowned worldwide as a place of violence and unrest. Israeli troops withdrew in May 1994 and the Gaza Strip became a self-rule area under the Palestinian Authority in 1994, with Yasser Arafat returning as its President. (Self-rule, however, only applies to the 60 per cent of Gaza not occupied by the Jewish settlers.)

A good first point of contact for organizing a visit to Gaza is the Middle East Council of Churches in Jerusalem. They work with their counterpart in Gaza, the Near East Council of Churches (NECC), who are the second largest relief agency in Gaza, after UNRWA, the United Nations Relief and Works Agency for Palestine Refugees in the Near East. They will co-ordinate your visit, set up meetings with local Christians and show you around the projects they run, including:

- A well-baby clinic, offering pre-natal and post-natal services. The mortality rate among infants in Gaza is about 30 per thousand, compared to less than 10 per thousand in Israel. The NECC also runs three health clinics with an emphasis on preventative care. Each health clinic services 20,000 people.
- Men's and women's vocational training centres. The men's centre teaches basic literacy skills, carpentry, furniture-making and metalworking. The women's centre teaches knitting, sewing, advanced dressmaking, computer classes and secretarial studies. Elderly women, widowed through the Intifada or the 1948 war, make uniforms for the men's vocational training centre. These centres are beacons of hope in an area of chronic unemployment.

The NECC or the Mennonite Central Committee in Jerusalem or World Vision in Jerusalem can also organize visits to:

- The Ahli Arab Hospital. This was founded by the Church Missionary Society in 1891. It is now run by the local Anglican diocese. Situated off the main Palestine Square, this is the only non-profit hospital in Gaza and is funded by different churches and Christian organizations. Muslims and Christians staff the hospital, providing a badly-needed facility to an area that statistically has only one hospital bed for every thousand people. A small Anglican church, on the grounds of the hospital, was repaired and re-consecrated in 1997.

Follow the walls from the Ahli Arab Hospital round either way to reach the fourth-century Greek Orthodox Church of St Porphyrios. It is in a narrow street in an area known as the Christian Quarter.

A project supported by World Vision and the Presbyterian Church (USA) and helped by the Gaza Baptist Society, is:

- The Atfaluna Society for Deaf Children. This school, called 'Our Children' in Arabic, was set up in 1992, and was the first institution in the Gaza Strip devoted solely to deaf education and services for the deaf. It offers vocational training programmes, making goods such as Palestinian embroidered photo albums or olive wood camels. Learn some simple sign language to communicate with the children.

• The UNRWA Embroidery Shop in Gaza City (see page 124) is worth a visit. It sells crafts made by women in the refugee camps, such as wall hangings, bookmarks and baby blankets. UNRWA runs fourteen women's programme centres offering training in trades and handicrafts. UNRWA began operations in May 1950 to give emergency assistance to the hundreds of thousands of Palestinians displaced by the 1948 Arab–Israeli conflict.

The NECC, the Mennonites and World Vision will organize visits to Gaza for around eight to ten interested individuals. They can also set up meetings with local Christians or arrange briefings from, for example, the Palestinian Centre for Human Rights or the Palestinian Authority.

Fish is good and fresh in Gaza! Enjoy a meal on the shores of Gaza, while looking out to the Mediterranean, and help support the local economy!

Contact points
Middle East Council of Churches' Jerusalem Liaison Office: tel. 02-628 4493, fax 02-626 4730
The Mennonite Central Committee in Jerusalem: tel. 02-582 8834, fax 02-582 5823
World Vision International in Jerusalem: tel. 02-628 1793, fax 02-626 4260

Christian celebrations

In the Holy Land, Christian celebrations of major and minor feasts and saints' days are held throughout the year. However, since most of the Orthodox churches use the Julian calendar, the Western churches use the Gregorian calendar and the Copts use the Coptic calendar, even celebrations of the same feast may not always occur on the same day. The best place to get accurate dates and times is the Christian Information Centre (CIC) at Jaffa Gate in Jerusalem. (See Where to go from here? on page 125.)

Some suggestions as to the most colourful celebrations are listed below.

Christmas/Epiphany

Many people have recited during their childhood the phrase 'Christmas comes but once a year'. In Bethlehem it comes three times a year, to say nothing of the little Christmases celebrated by travellers any time they happen to arrive. As early as 336, 7 January was observed in Bethlehem as the day of Christ's birth and baptism as well as the arrival of the Magi. The establishment of 25 December as Christmas or Nativity occurred in Rome as a way to oppose the pagan feast on that day of the 'Birth of the Victorious Sun' by the Christian celebration of the birth of the 'Sun of Righteousness'.

The combined celebration on 7 January was thereafter divided into two festivals – 25 December for the birth of Christ and 7 January for the baptism and visit of the Magi. This split was eventually accepted by the Eastern Churches (except the Armenians).

To add a complication, in 1582 Pope Gregory XIII reformed the Julian calendar and although the West gradually accepted the reform, some of the Orthodox Churches never adopted the so-called Gregorian calendar. These Orthodox church celebrations on fixed dates are now thirteen days later than the equivalent Western celebrations, with Christmas on 7 January and Epiphany on 19 January. The Armenians celebrate only the 19 January date, combining Christmas and Epiphany on one day.

The biggest public celebrations are on Christmas Eve (24 December and 6 January) rather than Christmas Day. The streets in Bethlehem, especially Manger Square, are decorated with strings of lights, flags and bows. A large Christmas tree, donated by a northern European country and decorated with lights, is often on display and the live trees just outside the Church of the Nativity are decorated. Choirs from around the world perform in the Square and young men form impromptu circles to dance the *dabka*, the Palestinian national dance. Many years, fireworks are set off after dark and coloured spotlights illuminate the buildings and the sky.

On 24 December at about 1.30 p.m. the Latin Patriarch is driven to Bethlehem from Jerusalem via Manger Street, Star Street and Star Square to Manger Square. Both Christians and Muslims gather to see him arrive. He is accompanied by the faithful plus Scout groups and bagpipe bands. You are welcome to join the procession or wait for it in front of the Nativity Church. In Manger Square, bands perform and the Patriarch is then accompanied into the church by local clergy and municipal officials. The Midnight Mass in St Catherine's church on Manger Square is broadcast around the world on television. To attend the Midnight Mass you must get tickets as far in advance as possible from the Franciscan Pilgrims' Office at the Jaffa Gate in Jerusalem or watch it on television in the Square or at home.

There are other services in a variety of languages, but for English speakers the possibilities in Bethlehem include a Protestant service late in the afternoon on Christmas Eve at the Evangelical Lutheran church (Christmas Church). The Anglicans in Jerusalem bring people for carol singing in late afternoon at the YMCA Shepherds' Field in Beit Sahour and in the evening on the roof of the basilica. Many other groups gather as well at the Fields of the Shepherds in Beit Sahour for services.

On 6 January (Orthodox Christmas Eve, old-style) there are four processions over the same route for the Syrian Archbishop, Coptic Archbishop, Greek Patriarch and the Ethiopian Archbishop. It is wise to ask at the Ministry of Tourism office in Bethlehem, since the times of these processions change from year to year. Again, the arrival in Bethlehem is heralded by bells ringing and the drum beats of the bands and you are welcome to join the processions following the route as above. Residents of Bethlehem turn out in their Sunday-best clothes, no matter what their denomination, and there is an air of festivity all over town. Some families have the custom of dressing their little children as monks or nuns so you are likely to see a miniature monk, complete with stove-pipe hat, brandishing a lollipop instead of a cross!

The Ethiopian Church's girls' choir comes in advance of the Archbishop and sings and moves with drum accompaniment on Manger Square. After the procession the Ethiopians go up to the Ethiopian Monastery of Peace – Church of Eyesus on Milk Grotto Street – for a series of services. The Syrians, Copts and Greeks hold liturgies in the Church of the Nativity in turn from late morning on Christmas Eve until about 3 a.m. on Christmas Day itself and there are sometimes fireworks after dark.

The Armenians have their procession on 18 January (Christmas Eve and Epiphany Eve). When the procession enters the Basilica of the Nativity, they turn to the right and go upstairs to the Armenian Monastery and only later hold a service in their area of the Basilica.

Holy Week and Easter

In the case of Holy Week and Easter, there are again two calendars to take into account but plans are being suggested to put an end to the split in the dates of Easter by the year 2001. That happens to be a year when both Eastern and Western Easters are on the same date – 15 April. The first Ecumenical

Council in Nicaea in 325 declared that Easter should be celebrated on the first Sunday following the first full moon after the spring equinox. The problem for the Orthodox is that the spring equinox is calculated according to the Julian calendar – that is, thirteen days after it actually happens. Once Easter is established, however, all the other dates in Holy Week and Lent fall into place.

For the time being, there are still two different Holy Weeks and Easters celebrated in the Holy Land with the exception of parts of the northern West Bank where they quietly celebrate the dates in common. The best thing to do is to get the schedule from the Christian Information Centre (page 125) and choose your services.

Palm Sunday, in all churches using the Western calendar, begins the week with services in the morning and a palm procession in the afternoon. The procession starts at the top of the Mount of Olives, goes across the Kidron valley to St Stephen's Gate and to the Church of St Anne where a short service of song and prayer is held. This is becoming an ecumenical procession with some of those using the Orthodox calendar processing as well. It is recommended that you join with a group singing in your own language since there is some friendly competition between groups and it is more fun to sing songs you know.

During the Western Holy Week there is a plethora of services to choose from. Most pilgrims and visitors go to services at several different locations rather than follow one calendar. The Franciscans lead a devotion on the Via Dolorosa on Good Friday and other groups walk and pray the route throughout the day. There is a Burial Service that evening at the Melkite (Greek Catholic) Church which many local people attend. Here the coffin of Christ is symbolically carried around the church and red and white carnations are distributed as a sign of mourning. This church continues using an Eastern rite but follows the Western calendar. On Saturday evening there are Easter Vigils at St Anne's and at Ecce Homo which include the affirmation of baptism and the Eucharist. They are exciting services beginning out of doors with the kindling of a new fire. On Easter Sunday morning, several groups gather at Augusta Victoria for a sunrise service and often there is an all-night vigil there on the hill. Easter services continue throughout the day. Many a visitor comes to the end of Easter with the quip 'I'm churched out!'

Eastern Holy Week begins with Lazarus Saturday, including a service on the Mount of Olives in the Tomb of Lazarus. Palm Sunday is celebrated with processions around the tomb in the Holy Sepulchre. Most groups celebrate Maundy Thursday with foot-washing, including a crowded Greek Orthodox service in the courtyard outside the Holy Sepulchre. The Armenian Orthodox service in the afternoon is less crowded and just as impressive. Processions along the Via Dolorosa and burial services mark Good Friday.

The highlight of the week for the faithful of the Greek, Armenian, Coptic and Syrian Orthodox churches is the Ceremony of the Holy Fire on Easter Saturday. The Holy Sepulchre is completely filled with people holding bundles of 33 candles to be lit by the Holy Fire. After processions and formal ceremonies, the Greek Patriarch and an Armenian priest or bishop are sealed in the edicule (tomb) until such time as a new fire is kindled and passed out through the holes on either side. The fire is passed rapidly from bundle of candles to bundle of candles, the bells ring and people cheer. The Holy Fire is then taken by air to Greece, as well as by runner or car to churches in Christian towns and villages where bells are rung continuously. The arrival of the fire in Bethlehem resembles the Christmas Eve processions with bands and cheering. The Greek Patriarch takes the flame into the Basilica of the Nativity and lights the hanging lamps and the candles of the faithful.

You can attend this ceremony in the Holy Sepulchre by waiting in the courtyard to get in or by getting permission to enter with one of the church's processions. And don't forget to buy a bundle of special candles in advance. The Ethiopian Orthodox hold a 'Resurrection Procession' with the singing of Easter hymns by candlelight on the roof of the Holy Sepulchre on the evening of Holy Saturday. Easter Day services in the Orthodox tradition begin early in the morning (1 or 2 a.m.) and by the time most

Western Christians are up, the Orthodox have gone to bed.

Another seasonal tradition is the eating of special Easter cookies. They are eaten by those celebrating either of the Easters as well as Muslims celebrating the end of Ramadan and nowadays they have been appearing around the Christmas season as well. Sometimes they are brought from one family to another as gifts. Known as *ma'mool*, they come in two forms – one stuffed with date paste and shaped like a crown, the other stuffed with chopped nuts and symbolizing either the sponge used to give Christ the wine vinegar or the rock in front of the tomb. Families and friends work together to make these treats since the process is long and the work needs many hands. Local Christian hospitality will keep you well supplied!

OTHER FESTIVALS AND EVENTS

1. *Assumption Day or Dormition of Mary (15/28 August)*

On the eve of the feast in Nazareth (14 August, Western calendar), celebrations begin with an evening procession (starting at 6 p.m.) of local Nazarenes, led by the town's Boy Scouts carrying an icon of the Virgin Mary through the streets. As the evening progresses, there is much singing and dancing, culminating in a fireworks display where the whole town is illuminated by colourful showers of exploding fireworks.

The next day, on 15 August, after 10 a.m. Mass in the Church of the Annunciation, the annual 'Dance of the Swords' takes place in the plaza outside the church. Sixty to seventy young men form a circle to dance around two Nazarenes, wielding swords and shields, symbolically acting out a battle between good and evil. The dancers chant their devotion to the Virgin Mary, promising to protect the Holy Mother with their blood and their lives and asking her to save them from evil. Good is ultimately declared the victor in the battle, Christianity victorious, and, amid exploding fireworks, the dancers lead the procession onto the streets once again.

In the Jerusalem area, Assumption day, 28 August, is a major feast day in the Orthodox church. In preparation, an icon of the Dormition of Mary is carried in procession from a chapel dedicated to the Virgin Mary, located on the parvis of the Holy Sepulchre, to the Tomb of Mary early in the morning of 25 August by the Orthodox clergy.

At 2.30 a.m. on 28 August the people of Bethlehem, mostly women, gather in groups in Manger Square as people assemble in other nearby towns. Some of these Orthodox faithful have fasted for fifteen days and some are prepared to walk barefoot to Mary's Tomb in Jerusalem. The walk is held in silent prayer at a steady pace with the object of arriving at Mary's Tomb before sunrise.

Some carry flowers, others sprigs of basil. A few carry a candle or oil in fulfilment of a vow. The route goes around the Old City walls to the Tomb where the walkers light candles on the steps leading down to the tomb and around the tomb itself. The flowers, basil and gifts are also placed around the tomb and an Orthodox liturgy is held. After the liturgy, the priests pass out blessed bread and the doors of the church are kept open 24 hours a day for the next seven days. On 5 September, the icon is returned in procession to the Church of the Holy Sepulchre.

2. El Khader Day (6 May)

No one knows if St George is a legendary or a historic figure; there is no absolute proof either way. It is said that he was born in Lod (south-east of Tel Aviv) in the late third century, killed the dragon at the entrance to that city, died and was buried there. The town of El Khader, just south of Bethlehem, is known as his place of imprisonment. Chains in the Greek Orthodox Church Convent are said to be those that bound him and they are believed to cure diseases, especially of the mental type.

The village of El Khader celebrates St George's Day on 6 May with both Christians and Muslims joining in the events. On 5 May there is a festive air with people bringing their picnic lunches and sitting under the olive trees. Since the building of the by-pass road in the area there are far fewer olive trees and fewer picnics as a consequence. People fulfil vows by bringing the gifts they had promised God. Muslims often sacrifice an animal or pour out oil while Christians bring gifts.

On 6 May, early in the morning, Orthodox lay Christians walk in silent procession from towns and villages in the Bethlehem area to the town of El Khader. (The procession is similar to the one on Assumption Day.) An Orthodox liturgy is held around 8.00 a.m.

3. Week of Prayer for Christian Unity (late January)

The Week of Prayer for Christian Unity is celebrated the world over in a variety of formats ranging from a single ecumenical service to services every day. In Jerusalem, the custom is to hold eight services in the late afternoon in each of eight churches, Sunday through to the following Sunday, mostly attended by Jerusalem Christians and expatriates. Usually the time is the last full week in January but the choice of week is dictated by the fact that the Orthodox churches celebrate 19 January as Epiphany and the Armenian Orthodox celebrate that date as both Christmas and Epiphany. By common consent the week begins after 19 January, even if it runs into February. A group called the Ecumenical Circle of Friends is the official facilitator of the programme in Jerusalem. Given the broad variety of churches and languages, the eight days provide a liturgical feast, especially for the local Christians.

4. World Day of Prayer (First Friday in March)

Each year, a group of Christian women gather and plan for celebrating the World Day of Prayer following the materials produced by an international committee. The liturgy is planned and written by women of a specific country and then translated into a variety of languages. In Jerusalem, an effort is made to include women of all ages and of as many traditions as possible. Recently, with some women clergy living in the city, the committee has been turning to them as preachers for the service.

5. Other celebrations mentioned in this book

4 August: St Mary Magdalen (see page 26)
10 August: Smolensk Icon (see page 26)
27 September: The Exaltation of the Holy Cross (see page 12)
4 October: St Francis of Assisi (see page 31)
17 December: Feast of St Barbara (see page 104).

Alternative shopping

Non-governmental organizations and church-related groups have been encouraging the revival of Palestinian crafts as a way of keeping the culture alive and providing income for Palestinian families. In the West Bank and Gaza there is very high unemployment and women without professional training can work at home, especially producing needlework and food. This work sometimes provides the only income for a family where the husband or father cannot get to his job in Israel. These goods are often far superior to the manufactured items available in the markets. Development projects, though, are only successful when there is an outlet for the work and when the producer receives a fair price. Fair trading is practised in all the outlets below. Enjoy your shopping!

One of the main outlets for good quality handmade crafts is at **Sunbula,** formerly **Craftaid,** at St Andrew's Hospice, near the railway station in West Jerusalem. It is open from Monday to Saturday from 9 a.m. to 6 p.m. and on Sunday from 11 a.m. to 1 p.m.

Sunbula means 'grain of wheat' in Arabic. With its biblical symbolism, it represents a lifeline to many Palestinians who are refugees or economically disadvantaged.

Its shop markets crafts from over 40 local Palestinian self-help groups in the West Bank and Gaza, from women's committees, centres for the handicapped, co-operatives and refugee camps. It encourages self-help groups, especially women's organizations, through marketing their products and developing management and promotional skills in the groups. It also promotes fair prices and quality work along with the encouragement of traditional crafts combined with modern materials and is a member of the

International Federation of Alternative Trade. Here, for example, you can find embroidered tablecloths, cushion covers or clerical stoles from the Surif Women's Co-operative near Hebron in the West Bank. There is also work from the Atfaluna Society for Deaf Children in Gaza or from the UNRWA embroidery projects for refugee women in Gaza or from the Pastoral Centre in Ramallah, run by the Greek Catholic Church. This centre employs up to 400 women, both Muslim and Christian, to embroider at home.

Sunbula also sells alternative Christmas cards with images of the birth narrative painted by a group of children aged between nine and twelve from Bethlehem and Jerusalem. The cards, and a compilation calendar, are the result of art workshops for both Muslim and Christian children in which the children were told the stories of Jesus' birth as represented in the Qur'an and in the Gospels.

Contact point *Tel./fax 02-672 1707*

Another good source of traditional Palestinian needlework is the **Arab Orthodox Women's Shop** at the **Melia Centre for Art and Training** in the old city of Jerusalem. It is on Frères Street, just down from New Gate.

Through the Women's Rehabilitation Programme (WRP), the Arab Orthodox Society has set up a programme to empower women through teaching knitting, crocheting, embroidery, fashion design and sewing. The shop offers both traditional embroidered items and newly designed clothes made by over 500 local women in their homes, and checked and supervised at the centre.

Some of the proceeds go to a health clinic run by the Society.

Contact point *Tel./fax 02-628 1377*

Next door is the Palestinian Coffee Room and Pie House, **Bint El Balad** ('the Country Daughter'). It is part of the same Arab Orthodox programme as above and was opened in 1996 to help teach food processing and the making of preserves and pastry and to be an income-generating project to economically disadvantaged women in the Old City.

Today, traditional Palestinian pastries and pies, with their distinctive blend of spices and nuts, are made by about twenty women in the Old City, supervised and quality-controlled in their own homes.

Palestinian women are proud of their food, which is as much a part of their national heritage and cultural identification as any other art form.

Stop to enjoy an Arabic coffee or fresh lemonade with some stuffed vineleaves, Armenian pizza, kubbeh or tabbouleh. The coffee shop is open from 8 a.m. to 7 p.m., Monday to Saturday.

Contact point *Tel. 02-626 0754*

The Palestinian Needlework Shop (Mennonite Central Committee building at 79 Nablus Road) sells needlework from a variety of women's co-operatives as well as cards and other local items. Much of it comes from Surif, near Hebron, and the Mennonite's Women's Co-operative, in the West Bank.

Around 400 women now run the Surif Women's Co-operative, originally set up by the Mennonite Central Committee after the 1948 war. Their traditional counted cross-stitch embroidery helps contribute to the family income while keeping the Palestinian heritage alive with patterns derived from village dresses and reflecting the traditions of varied regions of the country.

Brown, deep red and yellow are associated with Jerusalem, for example, as earth colours. Hebron and the Gaza Strip are identified by bright red colours and corn yellow is linked to the Ramallah region. The traditional red is associated with blood – the price of keeping the family honour and kinship intact.

The cross-stitch is said to have been created by Christian women, who based it on the sign of the Cross. Each thread is said to connect a woman's heart to her hands, as it weaves together generations – the past, present and future of Palestinian women.

Contact point *Tel. 02-582 8834, fax 02-582 5823*

At the **Anat Palestinian Folk and Crafts Centre** (in Beit Sahour near the Municipality Building), training courses are run for women and there is a market for handmade crafts along with a museum and demonstration centre. A phone call in advance is needed to ensure a guide or to request a light meal. As an environmentally-conscious centre, Anat pioneers recycling old needlework into new objects.

Contact point *Tel. 050-224 325 (mobile phone) or 02-647 2024*

The UNRWA Embroidery Shop in Gaza (Mustafa Hafez Street). This is the outlet for the handiwork produced by women of UNRWA agencies in Gaza. Look especially for the gold and brown embroidery on black cloth produced in that area.

Contact point *Tel. 07-677 7294/677 7333/282 4508, fax 07-677 7388*

Where to go from here?

Christian Information Centre

The most important source of detailed information for Christians is the Christian Information Centre on the plaza inside Jaffa Gate in Jerusalem. It has listings of the times of worship services, information about sites, institutes, libraries, social service agencies, Christian schools and Christian guest houses and hotels. It also has the dates of Christian, Muslim and Jewish feasts and festivals and just before Christmas and Easter special listings are published of the times and places of services.

Items for sale include religious and archaeological books, guide books for holy places and some of the best maps of Jerusalem. The centre is run by the Franciscans and staffed by a multilingual group of nuns who are very knowledgeable about the whole country. Additionally, at the same centre a service called the Franciscan Pilgrims' Office is run for Catholic priests who wish to say Mass in churches and holy sites. It is also the place to buy tickets for the Christmas Midnight Mass in Bethlehem.

Contact point *Tel. 02-627 2692, fax 02-628 6417, website: http://www.Christusrex.org/www1/OSM/CICmain.html*

Travel planning beyond the traditional tour

A number of non-profit organizations and church-related agencies are willing to be helpful if you contact them in advance. Do this as you begin planning your trip and before you sign up with a tour agency. They don't replace your travel agent, but they can help plan lectures, visits, seminars, briefings, and meetings with local Christians and human rights organizations. In co-operation with your travel agent they can help plan shopping stops at the outlets mentioned in the chapter on Alternative shopping. Since most of them help with travel in addition to other activities, make your contact early to be sure they can fit you in. A number of Christian or church-related organizations have recently formed a network called **al-Jisr**. *Jisr* in Arabic means 'bridge' and so the group hopes to act as a bridge to responsible Holy Land travel. Those listed below may be a good first point of contact in helping you plan your travel and set up meetings with local Christians.

Contact points
Augusta-Victoria Centre (especially for German speakers) (tel. 02-628 7704, fax 02-627 3148)
Catholic Relief Services, USCC (tel. 02-582 8149, fax 02-582 9280)
International Centre of Bethlehem (tel. 02-277 0047, fax 02-277 0048)
Mennonite Central Committee (tel. 02-582 8834, fax 02-582 5823)
Ecumenical Travel Services of the Middle East Council of Churches, Jerusalem Liaison Office (tel. 02-628 4493, fax 02-626 4730)
St Andrew's Scots Church (tel. 02-673 2401, fax 02-673 1711)
Swedish Christian Study Centre (especially for Scandinavians) (tel. 02-626 4223, fax 02-628 5877)

The **Alternative Tourism Group Study Centre** in Beit Sahour is not a specifically church-related organization but it plans tours which include meeting the Christian 'living stones'.

Contact point *Tel. 02-277 2151, fax 02-277 2211, e-mail: atg@p-ol-com webside: http://www.patg.com*

St George's College at the Anglican Cathedral in Jerusalem offers short-term courses, many of which include meeting local Palestinian Christians.

Contact point *Tel. 02-626 4704, fax 02-626 4703*

The **Sabeel Liberation Theology Centre** was founded in 1990. Sabeel is an ecumenical centre of Palestinian Liberation Theology which seeks to make the Gospel contextually relevant. In Arabic, *sabeel* means 'The Way' and also a 'spring' of life-giving water. Working from an old renovated Arab house at 13 Shimon Ha-Tsadik (close to the American Colony Hotel in East Jerusalem), it organizes programmes for adults and young people raising issues of justice and peace through youth camps, Bible studies, workshops and clergy gatherings. It can help organize meetings with local Christians to hear about their contemporary concerns. It also produces an English-language quarterly news-letter, *Cornerstone*, which presents theological reflections on contemporary social/political events.

Groups of friends of Sabeel operate in North America, the UK and Sweden.

Contact point *Tel. 02-532 7136, fax 02-532 7137, e-mail: sabeel@planet.edu   website: www.sabeel.org*

The **Jerusalem Liaison Office (JLO) of the Middle East Council of Churches** represents all four families of churches in the Middle East. It works to highlight the concerns of Christians of the Holy Land in international advocacy work and to further the unity of the Christian churches in the land itself as well as to enhance inter-faith dialogue with Islam and Judaism.

The *Ecumenical Travel Services* of the JLO can organize trips for small groups to settlements, refugee camps, to Gaza or the West Bank – so long as they are notified well in advance. They can also provide briefings on the situation of Palestinian Christians and meetings with local Christian groups.

The JLO also sponsors a wide variety of publications and organizes seminars and conferences to discuss issues of concern to local Christians from domestic violence to the role of the laity to the work of non-governmental organizations in the region. It produces a bi-monthly newsletter, *Kairos*.

Contact point *Tel. 02-628 4493, fax 02-626 4730*

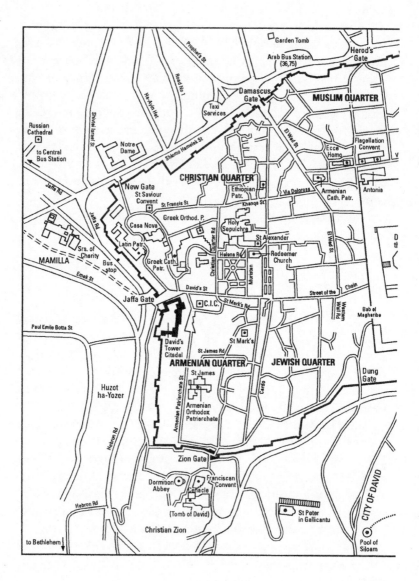

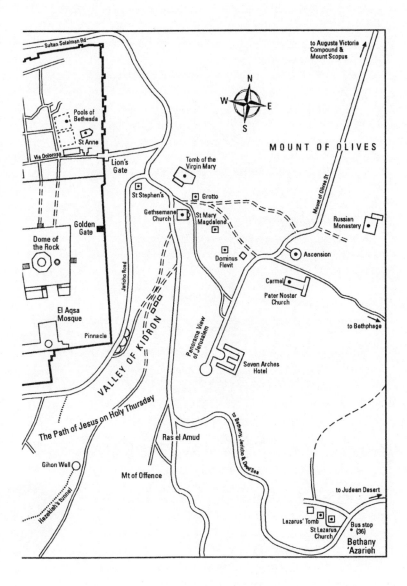

Sultan Soleiman Rd

Pools of
Bethesda

St Anne

Via Dolorosa

Lion's
Gate

Golden
Gate

Dome of
the Rock

El Aqsa
Mosque

Pinnacle

Jericho Road

VALLEY OF KIDRON

The Path of Jesus on Holy Thursday

Gihon Well

Hezekiah's tunnel

Mt of Offence

St Stephen's

Gethsemane
Church

Tomb of the
Virgin Mary

Grotto

St Mary
Magdalene

Dominus
Flevit

Panorama View
of Jerusalem

Ras el Amud

Seven Arches
Hotel

to Bethany, Jericho & Dead Sea

N
W   E
S

MOUNT OF OLIVES

Mount of Olives St

Russian
Monastery

Ascension

Carmel

Pater Noster
Church

to Bethphage

to Augusta Victoria
Compound &
Mount Scopus

to Judean Desert

Lazarus' Tomb

St Lazarus
Church

Bus stop
(36)

Bethany
'Azarieh

Stay With Me

Stay with me, re - main here with me, watch___ and pray,___ watch___ and pray.___

Music: Jacques Berthier
© 1978, 1980, 1981 Les Presses de Taizé (France).
International copyright secured. All rights reserved.

Jesus, Remember Me

Je - sus, re - mem - ber me when you come in - to your King - dom.

Je - sus, re - mem - ber me when you come in - to your King - dom.

Words from Scripture
Music: Jacques Berthier
© 1978, 1980, 1981 Les Presses de Taizé (France).
International copyright secured. All rights reserved.

Kyrie Eleison
Rabbana arhamna

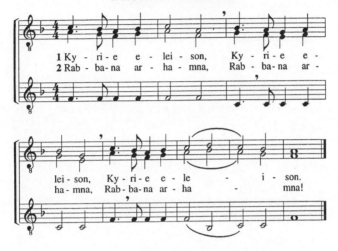

1 Ky - ri - e e - lei - son, Ky - ri - e e -
2 Rab - ba - na ar - ha - mna, Rab - ba - na ar -

lei - son, Ky - ri - e e - le - i - son.
ha - mna, Rab - ba - na ar - ha - mna!

1 = Greek
2 = Arabic
Words and music: Orthodox Liturgy from Ukraine.

O Lord, Hear My Prayer

(a) O Lord hear my prayer, O Lord hear my prayer. When I call an - swer me. O
(b) The Lord is my song, the Lord is my praise: All my hope comes from God. The

Lord hear my prayer, O Lord hear my prayer. Come and lis - ten to me. O
Lord is my song, the Lord is my praise: God, the well - spring of life. The

Words from Scripture
Music: Jacques Berthier
© 1978, 1980, 1981 Les Presses de Taizé (France). International
copyright secured. All rights reserved.

Lest We Forget Gethsemane

Lest we forget Gethsemane,
Lest we forget your agony,
Lest we forget love's victory,
Lead us to Calvary.

Words by Jennie Evelyn Hussey
Copyright © 1921, renewal 1949 by Hope Publishing Company
Administered by CopyCare, PO Box 77, Hailsham BN27 3EF,
UK. Used by permission.

This verse, the refrain of 'Ruler Of Life, We Crown You Now',
can be sung to 'Duncannon', the original melody for that hymn.
It can also be sung to 'Old Hundredth', 'Maryton' or 'Pentecost'
by simply extending the last line to read:

Lead us, lead us to Calvary.